Building Resilient Students

Integrating Resiliency
Into What You Already
Know and Do

D0002195

Kate Thomsen

Foreword by
Nan Henderson

CORWIN PRESS, INC.
A Sage Publications Company
Thousand Oaks, California

For information:

Corwin Press, Inc.
A Sage Publications Company
2455 Teller Road Thousand Oaks,
California 91320
www.corwinpress.com

Sage Publications Ltd.
6 Bonhill Street
London EC2A 4PU
United Kingdom

Sage Publications India Pvt. Ltd.
M-32 Market
Greater Kailash I
New Delhi 110 048 India

Printed in the United States of America

Library of Congress Cataloging-in-Publication Data

Thomsen, Kate.
  Building resilient students: Integrating resiliency into what you already know and do / by Kate Thomsen.
      p. cm.
Includes bibliographical references and index.
  ISBN 0-7619-4543-1 (C) -- ISBN 0-7619-4544-X (P)
  1. Educational psychology. 2. Resilience (Personality trait) in children. I. Title.
  LB1051 .T383 2002
  370.15´3--dc21
                              2002002765

This book is printed on acid-free paper.

            06 07 7 6 5 4 3 2

Acquisitions Editor:	Rachel Livsey
Editorial Assistant:	Phyllis Cappello
Production Editor:	Olivia Weber
Typesetter/Designer:	Siva Math Setters, Chennai, India
Indexer:	Teri Greenberg
Cover Designer:	Michael Dubowe
Production Artist:	Michelle Lee

Contents

Foreword

In my work training thousands of educators over the past decade—in the United States and other countries—I have seen the shift from self-esteem training to resilience training. There is a growing conviction that building resiliency in students is crucial to adequately prepare them for life in the 21st century.

What is fueling this migration to a resiliency approach? Mainly, it's happening because of the recognition that simply focusing on what is wrong with students does not produce the desired academic and behavioral outcomes. "People are more motivated to change when their strengths are supported," concludes Saleebey (1997, p. 13).

Educators tell me their students often go through a near-miraculous metamorphosis when the message "what is right with you is more powerful than anything that is wrong with you" (Henderson, 1999, p. vi) replaces the sense of inadequacy that is the unfortunate by-product of risk and deficit approaches. When students consciously understand how they have overcome challenges in the past and how they can use these same factors to overcome current life problems, a sense of self-efficacy emerges that is more potent than any other self-esteem building I have seen.

Building Resilient Students clearly shows that giving this gift to students does not involve adding one more thing to the plates of already overwhelmed educators. As the book carefully details, building student resiliency is integrally connected with the best educational approaches—many or all of which are already being used in schools. This book will give its readers a new set of glasses with which to view their work with students. Building resiliency, readers will learn, is not a program or curriculum per se but an attitude, philosophy, and set of strategies that can permeate everything an educator does—and fits best with the latest educational megatrends.

This book also provides educators with important validation and affirmation. They will see that what they do reaches far beyond what they suppose and will also see how their efforts in creating successful learners extend to providing a contribution to their students' resiliency that often lasts a lifetime (Higgins, 1994). And they will learn specific, detailed ways to be the most-effective resiliency builders they can be.

This is a book that should be read and embraced by all educators concerned that they not only help students learn the basics but that they also adequately prepare them for successfully meeting the challenges of life.

Nan Henderson, MSW
President
Resiliency In Action
San Diego, CA

Preface

Have you ever noticed that once in a while, a dandelion will plant itself in a very unlikely spot and begin to grow? I have seen abandoned parking lots filled with dandelions and weeds growing out of blacktop, not very fertile ground at all. Those dandelion seeds were blown by the wind and deposited randomly. Some landed on beautifully manicured lawns and others landed on paved roads. Because the seeds possessed everything that they needed to be the best dandelions possible, as soon as they landed, the seeds began to do what came naturally. Although the soil available was sparse, the seeds put down roots and began to grow in spite of landing in austere circumstances. That is because the environment had enough for growth to begin. As long as the rain came and the sun shone, the dandelions survived. However, if the parking lot began to have cars that ran over the plants, or if the rain didn't arrive and the sun shone too much, even the heartiest dandelions would succumb to their environment. So it is with people.

Unless there are extenuating physical circumstances, most of us are born with everything we need to grow into competent adults. We arrive in our environments, just like dandelions, without the luxury of picking the most nurturing one. We begin to do what comes naturally: eat, drink, sleep, learn, and grow. Like dandelions, we seem to make the most out of the resources we have. As long as our environments have enough to satisfy our needs, we will continue this process. However, if we are continually stressed or run over by our environments, even the heartiest will succumb. That is why the people who have responsibility for creating and sustaining the environments in which children land must be vigilant in making sure that all children have the opportunity to grow into the competent adults they are meant to be.

Educators create environments all the time—in classrooms, cafeterias, counseling centers, and even hallways. I believe that if educators understand and use resiliency-building concepts, school environments will improve, and schools will be better places for kids. All children who land in a classroom are capable of learning in their own ways, and every educator who interacts with a child needs to believe that and help that to happen. Educators need to guide kids to find their own resilience so that they can thrive no matter what their circumstances. The five specific educational topics, or megatrends, included in this book, are not only solid educational practice but also are integral to building resilience in students in the school setting. This book will make the connection between the five specific educational topics and resilience.

WHO IS RESPONSIBLE FOR BUILDING RESILIENCE IN STUDENTS?

Every adult who interacts with a child educates in some way. In a school setting, teachers, counselors, social workers, nurses, psychologists, clerical staff, and support staff are all role models and have the potential to impact a student's academic and social growth. These educators often feel the weight of the world on their shoulders and understandably so. In addition to their actual jobs during the school day, they may act as parent, counselor, disciplinarian, nutritionist, police officer, and friend to many young people. It is especially difficult to educate children in this day and age. Even though educators' jobs may seem almost impossible, the research on resilient people often reveals that a school experience or staff person had made the most significant difference in a young person's life (Benard, 1991).

WHO HAS THE TIME OR KNOWLEDGE TO DO THIS?

This book is designed to be a resource for busy educators who have little time to study. A great deal of information is summarized, and resources are provided for those who wish more in-depth information. Educators want to do the best for their students yet don't always feel that they can. Time constraints, few resources, more emphasis on higher standardized-test scores, and students with few family or community resources can make a difficult job even more challenging. Preservice education cannot possibly prepare professionals for everything they will need to know to do their jobs, especially the parts that deal with socioemotional issues. So once they are on the job, educators often attend inservice training. Some are designed to introduce new educational concepts and some to enhance the staff's ability to use complicated instructional approaches such as learning-style theory.

Educators often return to their work places and store volumes of new information in their files, which become like educational pantries. Staff development rarely comes with the follow-up and coaching that ensures its utility. So educators wait for a break in the action so that they may read the new information, process it, and put it to use. Often, the anticipated break doesn't arrive, and the very information that could make them more effective remains on the shelf. Without adequate knowledge, skills, and resources, many educators burn out. Burnout is not from working hard but, rather, from feeling ineffective.

USING RESILIENCY THEORY IS GOOD EDUCATIONAL PRACTICE

Resiliency theory and the strategies that emanate from it may be an answer to an educator's prayers. I have had students in my graduate class, who experimented with some simple strategies as part of their projects, tell me that the student response is immediate and positive. These teachers and counselors, some teetering on the brink of burnout, became excited because reluctant students finally responded to their efforts. I am convinced that students whose teachers use resiliency-building strategies act better and perform better both inside and outside school.

For many years now, information on building resilient students has been available to schools. I used to wonder why more schools were not embracing the resiliency concepts. I now realize that the reason may be that resiliency is perceived as additional information that cannot be attended to because educators are overwhelmed with so many new tasks and needy students. In addition, they are being asked to address issues of inclusion, learning styles, multiple intelligences, performance-based assessments, technology, higher standards, and more. In effect, their plates are full and their pantries are overstocked. As a result, resiliency is not receiving the attention it deserves.

Henderson and Milstein (1996) introduce the notion that good educational practice builds resilience. They identify how resiliency is related to current educational megatrends, such as the connection of learning to the real world or the involvement of all stakeholders in the solution of problems. I use their concept as a starting point in this book. I have identified five megatrends that are related to building resilience in students. These are: character education, multiple intelligences, emotional intelligence, service learning, and violence prevention. The resiliency wheel, which Henderson and Milstein (1996) developed to illustrate the six components of resiliency-building strategies, will feature prominently in this book. After the first chapter, which lays the foundation for understanding resiliency, each subsequent chapter will relate how resiliency is inherent in a particular megatrend. The wheel will be used to generate ideas and strategies for using each trend more deliberately to build resiliency. When resiliency is viewed as an integral part of good educational practice, it ought to feel less like one more thing to do (Henderson & Milstein, 1996).

VALIDATING THE ART OF TEACHING AND COMMON SENSE

While reading this book, educators may realize that they are already doing many resiliency-building things. For example, by implementing strategies for building responsibility through character education, educators are actually building resilient students. Also, when teachers recognize and use students' strongest intelligences, students learn better and feel more bonded to school. Research indicates that students who are connected to school seem to be more resilient (Hawkins, Catalano, & Miller, 1992). By devising ways to help students become emotionally literate, educators are not only enhancing their ability to learn but also preparing them for life. As we move through the book, more connections will become evident.

I hope that this book will validate, reenergize, and instill hope in overwhelmed and tired educators. Each chapter deals with one specific topic and, while the information is not exhaustive, it is enough to lay a foundation for practical understanding. Very often, once educators have enough information to understand a concept, they can begin to implement strategies right away. I have included ideas and activities in chapter sections called Try This Out. This book is designed to be a practical resource for new and veteran educators that will not wind up in their well-stocked pantries. I hope that its utility will cause readers to place it within easy reach so they can start cooking right away.

ACKNOWLEDGMENTS

I would like to acknowledge the many people who have helped me with this project. Thanks to my friends, Val S. and Carol M., and the other readers and reviewers who took the time to read my drafts and offer helpful comments. Thanks to the counselors in the Alcohol/Drug Abuse Prevention Education Program (ADA-PEP) for inviting me into their groups and classes, where I have learned so much. Thanks to my students for sharing your insights and experiences and for trying out the strategies that have been suggested in class. You have confirmed for me that this stuff really works.

A special thanks to the fine editorial staff at Corwin Press who assisted me with my first book.

A special thanks to Nan Henderson and Bonnie Benard for inspiring me many years ago. Thanks, Nan, for your support and generosity in encouraging me to build on your work with the wheel.

Another special thanks to Alan Goldberg, Professor Emeritus, for giving me the chance to develop and teach my course at Syracuse University. It all started there.

Thanks to Mike Dolcemascolo for his on-going support and for giving me the courage to approach Alan Goldberg with my idea in the first place.

Thanks to Beverly Title for giving me the idea to turn my course into a book.

Thanks to my angels on earth: Sue, Val, Tina, Roie, and a very special candelabra named Patty.

Thanks to my wonderful family for rooting for the kid sister.

A very special thanks to Rob Bocchino for being so generous with his time, his encouragement, his advocacy, and his knowledge.

The following reviewers are also gratefully acknowledged:

Rob Bocchino
Cofounder
Heart of Change Associates
Baldwinsville, NY

Ruth Harper
Associate Professor and Interim Department Head
Counseling and Human Resource Development
South Dakota State University
Brookings, SD

Steve Hutton
  Elementary Principal
  Beechwood Elementary School
  Fort Mitchell, KY

Rocky Killion
  Assistant Superintendent
  Lake Central School Corporation
  St. John, IN

Mike M. Milstein
  Partner, The Resiliency Group
  Professor Emeritus, University of New Mexico
  Albuquerque, NM

Dave Scheidecker
  Academic Facilitator
  Neuqua Valley High School
  Naperville, IL

Lisa Suhr
  Technology Teacher
  Sabetha Middle and High School
  Sabetha, KS

Rose Weiss
  Principal
  Cambridge Academy
  Pembroke Pines, FL

About the Author

 **Kate Thomsen** is the Supervisor of Special Programs for Onondaga-Cortland-Madison Board of Cooperative Educational Services (BOCES), Syracuse, New York. She is also an Adjunct Instructor at Syracuse University's Graduate School of Education and Counseling. As part of her responsibilities, she supervises the programs of 40 counselors in a school-based drug and alcohol abuse prevention program. She frequently offers workshops on resiliency and related topics. Kate is cofounder and cochair of a local coalition, Prevention Partners for Youth Development, which works to integrate youth development principles, especially resiliency and asset development, into all youth services in Onondaga County.

A secondary English teacher with a master's degree in Rehabilitation Counseling from Syracuse University and a CAS in Educational Administration from State University of New York at Oswego, she has spent her career working in both school and community agency settings. She draws on this experience to offer many ideas and examples for building resiliency in youth.

1

Resiliency: The Basics

Resiliency studies, in fact, offer evidence of what educators have long suspected and hoped: More than any institution except the family, schools can provide the environment and conditions that foster resiliency in today's youth and tomorrow's adults.

—Nan Henderson and Mike Milstein (1996, p. 2)

NAN HENDERSON AND THE RESILIENCY ATTITUDE

In 1998, when Nan Henderson came to our community to speak, I was immediately struck by the truth and utility of her words. She took us through an exercise during which we were asked to bring to mind a child we had concerns about. We divided a piece of paper into two columns, and on the left side, we wrote down the problems and challenges this person was facing. On the right side, we listed the positive things or resources that this child had. Needless to say, our left side list was considerably longer than our right. Through discussion, we began to see that the items on the left were of little value

1

to us except for diagnostic purposes. It was the items on the right that provided the solid foundation for building resilient youths.

That day, it was my nephew that I brought to mind, and I realized then that if I wanted him to be a resilient person, I had better work harder to find and bring to his attention the assets, or resiliencies, that he already possessed. In that way, he could use those strengths to help him overcome the challenges that I had identified. This experience helped me to see that I needed an attitude adjustment. Loving and worrying about someone isn't enough. I needed to find, focus on, and build with the positive things about this person. I needed to focus less on the problematic things. After all, we are much more than our problems. The good news is that I did get a new attitude, and I have seen the positive results. I have been a believer in the power of the resiliency attitude ever since.

As Henderson explained to us, educators are trained to seek out problems. It is our job to diagnose and remedy whatever the issue may be. It is no wonder we are so good at it, but it is time for a change. We need to shift our thinking from deficits to assets, from problems to solutions. If we consider that during 13 years of schooling, a student will very likely have spent 15,000 hours in classrooms, gyms, cafeterias, or auditoriums, we cannot help but see that the school experience is a powerful one. It will have a lasting impact on a young person, with both positive and negative outcomes. If educators possess the resiliency attitude, positive school experiences will be more likely to prevail.

ENTER HENDERSON AND MILSTEIN'S RESILIENCY WHEEL

Henderson and Milstein (1996) simply and practically apply their resiliency theory to both individual students and to the school environment as a whole, including educators themselves. Their resiliency wheel is illustrated in Figure 1.1.

Figure 1.1   The Resiliency Wheel

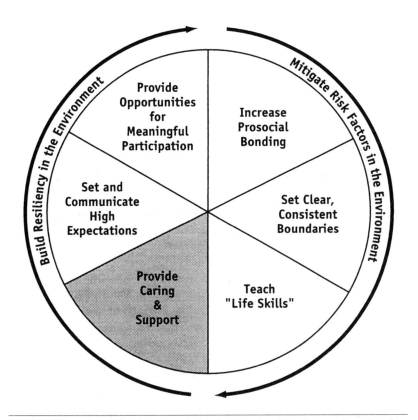

We will be using this wheel as we consider the five educational topics included in this book—one per Chapters 2 through 6. The left side of the wheel is the combination of the three elements for building resiliency identified by Benard in her synthesis of research on resilient people (p. 13), which we will address in greater depth in the next section. These elements deal with building resiliency in the environment:

Care and support include unconditional positive regard, support, and encouragement. This part of the wheel is critical because this is where relationships begin.

High expectations include making sure that young people know that we believe they can be successful as well as providing the resources for them to do so.

Opportunities to participate include giving young people opportunities to demonstrate their competence and willingness to contribute in meaningful ways.

Three more elements on the right side of the wheel are taken from the work of Hawkins, Catalano, and Miller, and illustrate the protective factors that they assert may mitigate risk (pp. 11-13) and deal with mitigating risk factors in the environment:

Prosocial bonding includes increasing positive connections between youths and their peers as well as between youths and the adults in their environments.

Clear boundaries and expectations include policies and rules that govern youths' behavior. They need to be fair and consistent and developed with youths' input.

Life skills include skills of decision making, communication, stress management, conflict management, and so forth. Schools need to prepare students for life after school.

By developing strategies based on all six elements, Henderson and Milstein (1996) believe that environments can be created that mitigate risk factors and promote resiliency. Using the wheel as a model, they provide examples of how students who need resiliency improvement might look and behave (Figure 1.2).

We have all known students who are described in this figure. Very often, we have been at a loss for how to help them. Henderson and Milstein's wheel suggests that by focusing on the area of the wheel that relates to the behavior, educators

Figure 1.2   Profile of a Student Needing Resiliency Improvement

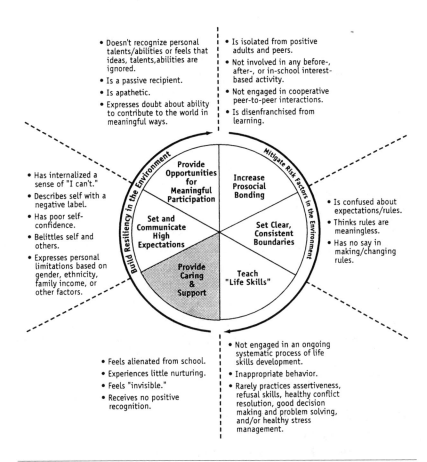

SOURCE: N. Henderson & M. Milstein, *Resiliency in schools: Making it happen for students and educators,* p. 21, copyright © 1996 by Corwin Press. Reprinted by permission.

will begin to understand why students feel and act the way they do. More important, educators will begin to see the things they might do to remedy the situations by considering how students who are *thriving* in the school environment might look and behave (see Figure 1.3). When educators see these two comparisons, it is easy for them to imagine strategies that could help remedy difficult situations. For example, a teacher might ask students who feel they have no say in what happens to them to participate in creating a policy for classroom management. A student who is not socially connected might be offered the opportunity to join a peer leaders group. Henderson and Milstein's (1996) work offers a practical resource for educators who wish to improve the quality of the classroom or school environments.

Using the Wheel

As we saw earlier in the chapter, the wheel is a useful tool for determining why a student may seem unmotivated or may be unsuccessful academically or socially. The Wheel helps to diagnose which issues may be the culprits and also helps to plan appropriate interventions.

Students who are isolated socially may need a teacher to create situations where they can be obviously successful so that the class views the students in a more positive light. This teacher may look for ways for these students to contribute in meaningful ways. Or maybe a teacher could offer an opportunity for prosocial bonding by asking such students to showcase an accomplishment no one knows about. I recently discovered that a very shy young man who is an easy target for ridicule is actually a very accomplished equestrian. Learning this raised him in my estimation, and I suspect that his peers would feel the same way if they knew.

Students who do poorly in spite of ability may have a difficult home situation for which they require caring and support. Maybe a little extra attention from the teacher or counselor would help.

A teacher may be teaching in ways that miss a student's learning style, such as relying heavily on verbal information when the student needs information to be presented visually. Find out how your students learn best. Give them a learning style inventory or a multiple-intelligences survey (see

Figure 1.3.   Profile of a Student With Characteristics of
Resiliency

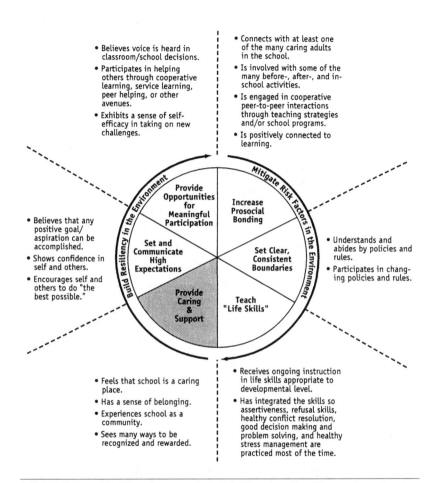

SOURCE: N. Henderson & M. Milstein, *Resiliency in schools:
Making it happen for students and educators*, p. 30,
copyright © 1997 by Corwin Press. Reprinted by
permission.

Resource A). Having high expectations for students must be
coupled with proper support, including assistance with organization and time management.

It isn't enough, however, to focus just on students in a school community. Schools that strive to graduate resilient students ought to be staffed with people who feel competent, capable, appreciated, motivated, and committed to their students. Since people cannot give what they do not have, it is imperative that administrators nurture their staff in the same ways that they seek to nurture students. On an airplane, the flight attendants remind adults to take their oxygen first before attending to their children. The same is true for schools. Principals and other administrators who interact with professional staff members would do well to consider the practical suggestions Henderson and Milstein (1996) offer for creating resilient staff, such as recognition for accomplishments or involvement in decisions that impact them. Just as the wheel is useful for students, it is also very practical for acquiring ideas and strategies for creating schools that create resilient staff.

I have presented Henderson and Milstein's resiliency wheel first in this chapter because it is the model that will be used throughout this book. However, to fully understand it and its origins, we will go back and fill in the theoretical foundations for understanding resiliency. To do this, I have summarized the main points of the following contributors to the resiliency movement: Bonnie Benard, Sybil and Steven Wolin, and Peter Benson.

FOUNDATIONS OF RESILIENCY

I was first introduced to the concept of resiliency in the early 1990s. My immediate response to the concept of resiliency was positive because it offers a different perspective on all youths and especially those we once considered to be at risk. Kids we believe to be at risk challenge us, ignore us, and often reject our attempts to motivate them. It is hard to think positively about these students. We may wind up avoiding them, even being secretly happy when they do not show up for school, so we can work with the more willing students. We could use a new perspective on them, and resiliency just might be it. Keep in mind, however, that the resiliency approach is not reserved for difficult students. It will benefit all students and most adults as well.

Resiliency theory asserts that there are seeds of resilience within each person, and outward appearances or behavior should not blind us. I have seen resiliency defined in many different ways, but, essentially, it is a person's ability to remain steady or to bounce back in spite of adversity. Resilient people draw on strengths, both internal and environmental, to overcome challenges. Often, resilient people have no idea that they are resilient. They simply do what needs to be done. They tap into an inner sense or wisely use resources, including other people, to help them survive and even thrive. Observers have learned a great deal from the behavior of survivors, and this knowledge can be applied not only to students from high-risk environments but also to all of our students.

Teachers and other educators who truly believe that, beneath the armor that protects some students, a good, capable person resides inside, look for the seeds of resilience until they find them. I have observed many kids from high-risk environments display negative coping behaviors that they may have learned in order to survive. Educators may need to help these young people redirect their skills into more positive endeavors, but first they must recognize the strengths that these kids possess. Once they do, giving up on a child becomes impossible. The resiliency approach is a hopeful one, and I believe that if educators feel hopeful about their students, their students will feel hopeful about themselves and their futures.

Resiliency theory comes from a body of information that was gathered from studying people in a different way. For many years, researchers studied people and their problems to learn what could be done to assist them and others like them. This *retrospective* research provided information about what people are like after problems have been present for a period of time. Researchers like Rutter (1984) and Werner and Smith (1989) undertook long-term, *prospective* research techniques. They studied people over many years. Some of those studied were from very high-risk environments and were expected to do poorly. The researchers saw that some did quite well in spite of negative circumstances and even negative prognoses. They wondered why these people were able to succeed when others from similar circumstances failed. They focused on their subjects' personal characteristics and their environmental influences. Until people who had overcome adversity were studied, no one knew what set them apart from the others. Now we do. Research on what internal and external factors seem to create resilient people shows us what actions we might take to help young people prepare for successful lives.

Anyone Can Be From a High-Risk Environment

Many students within our schools are from high-risk environments. It is easy to assume that the term *high-risk* means impoverished, but some of the most needy students are from affluent backgrounds. The term *high-risk* is very broad and can be interpreted in many different ways. I believe that there are times when being deprived of emotional support is far more painful than being deprived of material support. Many students, regardless of economic status, have little interaction with adult role models. Some live with addicted parents, and some have no clear boundaries or expectations in their homes and communities. Some are used to taking a back seat to their parents' interests. These students often present challenges in the school setting due to low motivation or negative behavior. These are the students who respond very well to resiliency-building strategies.

One resiliency-building strategy is giving kids an opportunity to contribute to causes or to serve others. I have seen disruptive students, who drain teachers' energy and patience, turn into gentle and caring people during service learning experiences when they interact with nursing-home residents or work with much younger students. Doing this type of activity requires planning and additional effort for teachers, but it is well worth it. In the different setting that service learning provides, students are free to be the persons they really are, not just learners in a classroom. It is empowering for students to be able to show that they can be competent in other ways. An additional benefit is that students who are actively and emotionally engaged in service projects can extract meaning and can even more easily apply many related concepts that teachers are trying to teach, such as citizenship or social responsibility (Krystal, 1998/1999). In the long run, students are more engaged in their learning and more likely to do well overall. In Chapter 5, we will look more closely at service learning.

Time to Question Our Attitudes

Whether or not the seeds of resiliency get nourished and grow often depends on the people surrounding a child and their attitudes toward children. In order to use resiliency concepts, we must be keenly aware of our mind-sets regarding all children. Do we really believe that poor kids with little parental involvement can succeed? Do we resent the affluent students who have every new gadget and drive cars newer than ours? Do we pay more attention to the kids whose parents watch our every move? Do we let the kids with poor attitudes vegetate because it is easier than challenging them to do well? Do we lower our expectations when working with children from economically disadvantaged environments because we want to "help" them be successful? Do we think it is important for our students to see us as real people with real problems, or are we supposed to be above all that? Do we ever consider that a child enters school each day carrying the baggage from the night before? As we think about these questions and consider our answers, our attitudes begin to reveal themselves. The resiliency movement is offering ways to develop a positive attitude toward all students.

People with the resiliency attitude see youths as resources instead of liabilities. They look beyond outward appearances and believe that there is a capable person inside. They are not afraid of adolescents but, rather, try to understand them by developing a relationship with them and creating a place where students can be safe to be themselves, where expectations and boundaries are clear. They remember their own youth and respect the changes all children must endure on their way to adulthood.

Good teachers have been building resiliency in students, without calling it that, since education began. Skilled teachers know how to relate to kids to determine what motivates them. They know how to identify strengths and build on them. Students of these skilled teachers emerge from their classrooms believing in themselves and being hopeful about their futures. Could it be that good teaching is just good old common sense? Maybe so, but, as my mother used to say, "Common sense isn't so common!" Teachers like this are a precious commodity.

If we reflect on our own educational experiences, we are very fortunate if we can recall even one teacher like the ones mentioned above. If we can, we might remember a person who saw our talents and encouraged us to achieve our potential. Maybe it was someone who appreciated our humor or thought we wrote well. Maybe it was a person whom we could talk to and whom we could trust. Such people undoubtedly possessed the resiliency attitude, meaning that they could see us as competent adults in the making and wanted to be part of our process. Unfortunately, in this day of higher standards and test results, educators are stretched for time and must focus on students' academic problems and their remediation rather than on discovering their interests and inspiring in them a love of learning. It seems that there is little opportunity to get to know students as individuals. A cycle of mutual anonymity often results, making it almost impossible to build relationships. It doesn't have to be this way.

The resiliency movement is attractive because it has identified the experiences and personal traits of those who overcame adversity. Logically, in order to enhance others' chances of becoming resilient, it seems we ought to recreate those same experiences and develop those traits more deliberately. While the research encourages focusing on home and community as well as on the school, it is common for schools to bear the heaviest burden (Benard, 1991). They are often the safest, most orderly and predictable places in a child's life. They are the places where hope in one's future can be born or destroyed. While home, school, and community all share responsibility for our youth, ensuring that students experience and benefit from good educational practices is the contribution schools can make so that students become resilient people. Youths with belief in their abilities and hope in their futures can overcome great adversity, including a bad home life (Benard, 1991; Peele, 1986). We have the tools to help them to believe in themselves. We just need to use them.

We are lucky today, in spite of all the pressures on educators. There is so much to help us to inspire kids. We are learning a great deal about how the brain works. We know there are many ways to be smart. We know that kids who have solid interpersonal skills will do better in life. We know that all kids don't learn the same way. We just don't know where to start as we try to incorporate this knowledge. It is a tall order. I hope this book will help.

OVERVIEW OF BONNIE BENARD'S MODEL

> Shifting the balance or tipping the scales from vulnerability to resilience may happen as a result of one person or one opportunity. (Benard, 1991, p. 15.)

Benard's (1991) seminal article cites approximately 122 sources and provides us with an overview of research that led to the concept of resiliency. Drawing on the work of notable researchers such as Werner and Smith, Rutter, Garmezy, Anthony, and Cowen, Benard is able to identify and explain similarities among their findings. The subjects studied came from various high-risk backgrounds and circumstances, and some did well in spite of it all. This research showed that there are both constitutional and environmental factors that account for the subjects' resiliency. Constitutionally, resilient people seem to have some internal, or dispositional, advantages in that they are easygoing and can elicit positive responses from others. These and the other internal characteristics that can be developed with additional assistance are summarized in Box 1.1.

Environmentally, resilient people seem to have had many similar experiences that kept them strong during difficult times. Sometimes these people were the caretakers of others. Younger siblings or older relatives may have depended on them. Those who were resilient felt that they were necessary and viewed themselves as capable people. They may have been involved in activities that cultivated their talents and provided them with an escape from a bad homelife. Overarching all this is the fact that during the growing years, resilient people had at least one very positive relationship with a significant adult who positively influenced their self-concept and decision making. This adult was not always a parent but was often an extended family member, sibling, youth worker, teacher, counselor, or neighbor.

Pines (1984) wrote about the research done by Rutter on the female offspring of severely mentally ill women. Rutter's long-term study showed that after 14 years, one third of the 89 young women followed were considered to be functioning well in spite of the severe circumstances in which they grew up. They were the resilient ones. Rutter looked for what protected these young people. Rutter said,

> So we looked to see what kinds of things had made a difference. And one thing was positive experiences at school. . . . These positive experiences were usually not academic success, but success in sports, achievement in music, getting positions of responsibility in the school (from classroom monitor to team captain), having a good relationship with a teacher, or sometimes just social success. (cited in Pines, 1984, p. 35)

Box 1.1

PERSONAL CHARACTERISTICS OF RESILIENT
PEOPLE

Nature

- **Having an easy temperament or disposition.** Some people are just naturally more flexible and easygoing than others. Babies show different personalities right away.

- **Having the ability to elicit positive response from others.** These are the people who are likable, friendly, and whom others want to be around. Often, these are natural leaders. While some people may learn techniques for successful social interaction, this ability is usually an innate characteristic.

Nurture

- **Having empathy and caring about others.** Babies are born with empathy (Goleman, 1995). However, it can be quickly forgotten if it is not nurtured in the environment. Luckily, it can be relearned through experiences.

- **Having excellent communication skills.** These skills include the ability to express one's needs and get them met, the ability to assert without becoming aggressive, the ability to resist pressure to do negative things, and so forth.

- **Having a sense of humor about one's self.** People who can see the humor or irony in situations that also bring pain are in a better position to recover from that pain. People who do not take themselves or their situations too seriously can see beyond the difficulty they are experiencing to a more hopeful future.

(continued)

Box 1.1 Continued

- **Having a sense of one's identity.** People who understand and take pride in their roots can use that knowledge to overcome adversity.

- **Having the ability to act independently.** People who take initiative and carry on with important tasks without having to rely on others are more resilient.

- **Having the ability to separate from unhealthy situations or people.** Very often, people who perceive themselves as different from those who are having a negative effect on them are able to make plans to do things differently in their own lives. This includes being able to think reflectively about a situation and resolve to do things better.

- **Having a sense of purpose or future.** People who feel that they are necessary to others because they are part of a family or social structure have a purpose in life. Believing that you can have a positive future in spite of current circumstances is enough to keep resilient people engaged in working toward that positive future. This may be the most important characteristic of all because people who believe in something bigger than themselves can often overcome great adversity. (Frankl, 1959)

For many of us, the obvious truth behind this clue to resiliency jumps out at us. Success breeds success, and children who are successful in at least one area can use this experience as a lifeline when times are tough outside school. Most educators can think of at least one child who hangs around the school or around a teacher, staying behind and looking for something to do, not wanting to go home. Children who successfully seek out and receive adult attention are exhibiting resilient behavior. We ought to nurture these seeds.

The next time we see this type of behavior, we might try to understand it from the resiliency perspective: a resilient child seeking to bond with a positive adult role model rather than a needy child seeking attention. We ought to be honored if we are the one sought after and look for ways to connect with such children so they can continue to grow into competent adults. Children often connect to something in us that we may not even know we have. If you are sought after, feel proud. If you see others being sought after, look to see what qualities they possess and see if they are ones you could emulate.

Benard (1991), for example, is one source of hope for many of us working with troubled and struggling youngsters. What has to be done to help kids grow into competent, caring adults is clear, in part, because researchers have studied people who have overcome adversity and written their conclusions about how these people came to be called resilient. Such research suggests ways to reach the kids who seem to be immune to interventions.

Kids from high-risk environments need us more than ever. Providing lessons in school on the dangers of drug abuse or giving kids an opportunity to discuss their problems in small groups is just not going to be enough. If we want to raise a generation of healthy, competent youths, we have to do much more. Every adult who interacts with young people in some way has to take ownership in this process.

Benard's (1991) conclusions are quite simple but not easy: The key to building resilient youths is through building caring and supportive relationships with them. Ideally, if we want to build resilient kids, we have to focus on the three most important environments in which a child lives, plays and works: namely, the home, school, and community. In those areas, three very important activities ought to be occurring. These are (a) the provision of a caring and supportive environment, (b) high expectations for each individual and the support to achieve them, and (c) opportunities for kids to contribute in meaningful ways. Figure 1.4 illustrates these points.

Specific strategies for addressing each segment of this model can be developed and used by adults in the home,

Figure 1.4   Keys to Building Resilient Youths

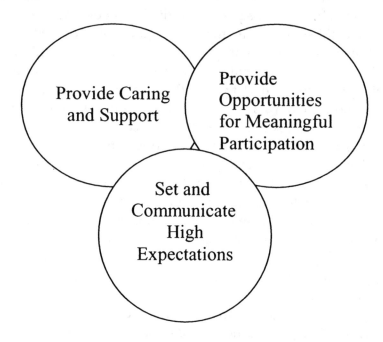

school, and community. The more often these strategies are used, the better chance kids have of growing into healthy, competent adults. The model uses overlapping circles because when an adult, parent, or other caregiver consciously creates an environment where these three strategies are employed, interrelationships will occur. Offering kids opportunities to contribute in meaningful ways communicates to children that they are important, capable, and necessary. This reinforces the care and support that the adult offers the child and, simultaneously, communicates to the child that this adult has high expectations based on a belief in the child's abilities.

Adults Hold the Power

The central concept in Benard's model is that adults have the power and responsibility to create environments where children can thrive. Children are born into their circumstances, they do not choose them. Adults (parents, teachers, neighbors, daycare providers, et al.) create environments in which children live, play, and learn until they are old enough to leave. In an ideal world, adults who love them and believe in them would surround all children. Homes, schools, and neighborhoods would be safe, and all children would be able to have their needs met in positive ways.

This is, however, not an ideal world. Many children are not lucky enough to be born into loving, stimulating homes. They may be unsafe in their communities. They may be at high risk in the school setting due to learning differences or poor social adjustment. They may find themselves in situations that place them at great risk for being damaged by others. Those of us who wish to positively impact the lives of children need to pay close attention to the environments we create. As adults, we have the power to create environments that will nurture or harm. It is our choice. Research indicates that if a child is born into less than ideal circumstances, a caring adult or positive experiences in other environments may override the child's negative surroundings (Benard, 1991). Since it is becoming less likely that youths will find safety and connection in their neighborhoods, schools may be the most consistent, safe places a child knows.

Tables 1.1, 1.2, and 1.3 list characteristics of three settings—home, school, and community—that make them resiliency-enhancing environments. They are based on Benard's (1991) model. (These characteristics are the basis for specific actions that adults might take in each setting.)

The lists in these tables are by no means exhaustive. They can easily be adapted either to plan an intervention for an identified child or to plan the creation of an ideal environment for groups of children, such as for a classroom or family environment. The more often that environments include characteristics from the three lists, the better able students are to develop resiliency.

Table 1.1   Characteristics of Homes That Build Resilience

Support and Caring	High Expectations	Opportunities to Participate
Positive, long-term relationships between adults and youths	Parents or other caregivers who believe in the youths' abilities	Children who participate in the household in meaningful ways, such as chores, caring for elders or younger siblings
Routine family activities, such as religious services, dinner, and so forth	Structure, order, and discipline with logical, fair consequences	Children who learn skills from adults that make them feel worthy and capable
Rituals and family traditions, such as birthday celebrations, holiday traditions	Clear boundaries which are enforced	Children who have a voice in family decisions
Supportive parents and siblings who celebrate one another's accomplishments	Mutual respect between parents and children	
Positive role models for responsible alcohol use or abstention, stress management, conflict resolution, and so forth		

OVERVIEW OF THE WOLINS' MODEL

Another very useful resiliency approach was put forth by Wolin and Wolin (1993) and is based on their own work with resilient clients. Unlike Benard, who synthesized and wrote about others' research, the Wolins wrote about their own

Table 1.2   Characteristics of Schools That Build Resilience

Support and Caring	High Expectations	Opportunities to Participate
Principals, teachers, and support staff who communicate concern for the whole child	Teachers and staff who believe, and behave as if, all students have potential	Roles and jobs for students that are valued and meaningful
Mechanisms for student support, such as newcomers' groups, Banana Splits, peer leadership, and so on	An academic climate that has both high expectations and adequate support	Ways for students to shine in addition to academics and athletics
Resources available for youths, both for academics and personal growth	Children who internalize high expectations for themselves	Students who are involved with service-learning
Staff members who avoid labels	Tutors and other support staff so that students can be successful	Students who volunteer in school and community
		Peer mediation for students

experiences and research. They developed a theory based not only on observations of their patients but also on much of the same research that Benard cites, especially that of Werner and Smith (1989) and Garmezy and Rutter (1983). In fact, following Garmezy's lead, the Wolins show us the flip side of the coin. They reframe a person's pain and strife to reveal resilience.

Steven Wolin practiced as a psychiatrist in the traditional medical model for many years. In this model, the therapist or doctor makes a diagnosis, labels the disorders and, through therapy, prescribes behavioral and pharmaceutical interventions. The patient is perceived as ill and powerless. The therapist shows the patient how to become well again. After many years of using this model, Wolin became dissatisfied and began to focus more on his patients' strengths. He specifically

Table 1.3   Characteristics of Communities That Build Resilience

Support and Caring	High Expectations	Opportunities to Participate
Availability of resources, such as mental health counseling, occupational assistance, youth programs	Youths who are seen as resources	Roles and responsibilities for youths
	Communities that give clear messages about acceptable behavior	Youths who are asked for their help and ideas
Social and recreational networks for youths and adults	Adults who set and model standards for positive community norms	Adults who show youths how to do important tasks, such as how to open a bank account or change a car's oil
Social supports across the life span	Adults who enforce policies and laws fairly and who offer logical consequences for rule infractions	
Adults who value and enjoy kids		Mentoring programs
Adults who provide mentoring and guidance for all youths, not just their own		Jobs for youths
Adults who advocate for kids	Adults who monitor media and advertising messages targeted toward youths	

noted and recorded behaviors that served these individuals well in spite of their adversity. Steven Wolin and his wife, Sybil Wolin, who holds a PhD in child development, grouped and eventually named these resilient behaviors, arriving at seven resiliencies (see Box 1.2).

In addition, they developed a model for working with people that they named the Damage versus Challenge model. The Damage model sees people as the medical model does, damaged and in need of repair. The Challenge model views people as having had experiences that were damaging but that, in effect, may have made them stronger. An arm that has

---

Box 1.2

THE SEVEN RESILIENCIES

1. **Insight:** The habit of asking tough questions which pierce the denial and confusion in troubled families

2. **Independence:** Emotional and physical distancing from a troubled family which keeps survivors out of harm's way

3. **Relationships:** Fulfilling ties to others that provide the stability, nurturing, and love that troubled families do not give

4. **Initiative:** A push for mastery that combats the feeling of helplessness troubled families produce in their offspring

5. **Creativity:** Representing one's inner pain and hurtful experiences in art forms—"building a new world on the ruins of the old"

6. **Humor:** The ability to minimize pain and troubles by laughing at oneself

7. **Morality:** An informed conscience which imbues the survivor surrounded by "badness" with a sense of his or her own "goodness"

SOURCE: Wolin and Wolin (1993).

---

been broken usually heals stronger where the break occurred. Similarly, the challenge model acknowledges the damage a person has suffered, but it looks for the strength that led to survival in spite of it. The Wolins acknowledge that all of us are a combination of our past pain, struggles, and strength— and our current pain, struggles, and strength. In fact, if we did not have adversity in our experience, we could not consider ourselves to be resilient. Once we become cognitively aware of what we have done to survive, or how we are resilient, we can incorporate that information into our self-concept. Their videotape series (Wolin & Wolin, 1994) *Survivor's Pride* offers wonderful illustrations of how people can come to see their own resilience and have pride in what they were able to accomplish.

According to the Wolins, in order to use the Challenge model, it is necessary for the counselor or teacher to possess three things:

1. The mindset that focuses on finding a person's strength rather than weakness—for example, recognizing that a child of an addicted parent is capable of getting to school each day in spite of the parent's neglect

2. The vocabulary of resilient behaviors—for example, knowing that the child's getting to school reflects initiative and ability to be independent

3. The ability to assist people in reframing their painful experiences—for example, helping this child to see that while the parent has an illness, the child does not and can make good choices that will help in leading a healthy life

I believe that this model is most useful in counseling situations, but some of the same techniques can be used by teachers and other educators who wish to look for ways to reframe children's difficulties so that they can view themselves as empowered and capable rather than victimized. The next section elaborates on this technique.

THE CHALLENGE MODEL AS IT RELATES TO BRIEF SOLUTION-ORIENTED THERAPY

In the counseling situation, the Wolins' model is similar to brief solution-oriented therapy, in which the focus is placed on what is going right and not on what is going wrong. In brief solution-oriented therapy, the person being counseled is an active participant in creating the solution to the problem being addressed. In traditional models of counseling or problem solving, the focus is on the problem. The problem is defined, examined, and energy is spent understanding the problem. Little or no attention is paid to the problemless state. The times when problems are not present are called exceptions (O'Hanlon & Davis, 1989).

In the brief-solution approach, attention is turned to the times when things go right or when there is no problem. That way, the brain begins to scan for positive experiences or circumstances rather than negative ones. When troubled students approach with a problem, a teacher or counselor might ask questions such as, "When you and your friends are getting along, what is happening?" Or "What is Miss Jones doing when you feel happy in her class?" Or "What were you doing in Miss Jones's class when she was not mad at you?" The student reflects and is actively engaged in creating the solution to the problem. By focusing attention on the times when things are going well, the student can become cognitively aware of useful behaviors and understand which behaviors can lead to problems. Once students are consciously aware of their actions and the consequences, their useful behaviors are more likely to become a solid part of their repertoire to be used in future situations. In focusing on what they are doing right, students no longer are victims stuck in problem-focused thinking but, rather, problem solvers focused on moving through problematic situations.

Youngsters who are used to dwelling on their problems are at a loss for words when teachers or counselors ask, "What went right for you today?" and then add, "Wow! How did you manage to do that?" Taking attention away from whatever is wrong is foreign to most youths used to talking about and dwelling on complaints and worries. It is a resiliency-building approach that at first will seem very strange to teachers, counselors, and students. However, it is an approach that is empowering to everyone involved. We often forget that the solutions to students' difficulties always rest within themselves. Because we forget, when students come to us with issues, we accept the role of the problem solver and quickly become overwhelmed with the problems that they face. The resiliency-building approach is a tool to assist students in finding their own solutions. It sounds so simple, but having youths focus on the effective things they have done is a powerful way to build their self-efficacy. The child is compelled to become self-aware or to be cognizant of effective actions. In this way, the actions can be stored in a bank of useful behaviors to be drawn on in the future.

Flipping the Coin

Using the Wolins' model, the counselor or teacher listens to what is being said and then helps the child to identify which behaviors have been effective. For example, if a child is struggling with family problems but still gets to school and makes it to class, it would be far better to point that out rather than to focus on what is not being accomplished. When you say something like, "You know, in spite of what is going on at home, I've noticed that you get here every day and make it to all your classes. How do you manage to do that?" the student is compelled to reflect on, and become cognitively aware of, what it takes to accomplish this. Once this has been expressed, you can add: "That shows me you are a responsible person and are motivated to do your best." While this interaction will not solve students' problems at home, it puts their effective behaviors in the forefront of their minds rather than their problems. As important, students will undoubtedly reflect on the fact that a teacher cares enough to ask them how they are doing and considers them to be responsible and motivated.

Acknowledging and reframing a person's actions, naming the person's effective behavior, and verbally presenting it is very much like giving a gift. One is not always aware of one's own efficacy until another makes it real by naming it. Once the awareness occurs, this knowledge can become part of one's self-image. The student mentioned above will begin to construct a self-image of a responsible person with motivation. The chances of this student's continuing to get to school are greatly enhanced now that a significant, caring adult has given this feedback. When times are tough and giving up looks like a good option, this student will likely remember this conversation and, hopefully, stay the course.

When young people are going through difficult times, they often get discouraged and feel as though no one understands. They may be drawing on great inner strength and not even know it. An adult who points out resilient behavior is helping children to create pride in their ability to survive. One counselor told me a story of a sixth-grade girl who was in her Banana Splits group, which is a small discussion group for students struggling with the divorce or separation of their parents. This girl was having difficulty staying awake in school and had not been doing very well. In group one day, she revealed that her mother had had another baby. That meant that there were now four younger siblings in the home. The tired, single mother refused to get up in the night to feed the baby, so this young girl was getting up to get the bottle for the new baby. Later, she made sure her younger sister got up and dressed for school, and then she went to school herself.

In the Damage model, this girl would have been seen as the victim of a mother who was robbing her of her childhood. In the Challenge model, this girl is seen as a dependable, empathetic, loving sister who knows the right thing to do. While both may be correct, pointing the latter out to her so that she can make it part of her self-concept is far more useful to her than dwelling on the unfairness of the situation. In this instance, the counselor does not suggest that her situation is fair or right. In fact, the counselor must acknowledge this child's struggle in order to validate her. Acknowledging pain is not the same as dwelling on it. A challenge mindset allows a person to move forward rather than to get stuck.

Empowering the Child Is the Adult's Role

A counselor or teacher who empowers a child with insight and skills is encouraging another resilient behavior, *adaptive distancing*, to take place. In adaptive distancing, individuals understand that the problems they are dealing with are not of their own creation. They are able to put distance between themselves and the people or situations that are causing pain. They understand that they did not create these situations and cannot fix them. They can, however, cope with them and emerge stronger for it. For example, children who return each day to homes where parents abuse alcohol or other drugs usually learn to live in chaos. They can count on very little consistency, and life is usually crisis management. With guidance from counselors and teachers, these children can learn about the disease of addiction and understand that they can make very different choices in life. They can learn to protect themselves emotionally and even have some insight and compassion for their parents. These children can be encouraged to join after-school activities such as sports or drama. If those options are not available, they can be encouraged to stay focused on academic goals. The important thing is that they stay busy and focused on bettering themselves and managing the chaos at home as well as possible until they are old enough to leave. Very resilient children often observe the behavior of the adults in their lives and resolve to do things differently when they have the opportunity. With assistance from other caring, adult role models, these children can love their parents but not their parents' behavior.

We should never gloss over or ignore problems that are placing our students at risk of harm. However, it is often impossible to correct poor home or neighborhood situations, and kids will have to endure difficult times. Rather than labeling them as damaged and pitying their lives, it is far better to reframe these students' challenges. Naming the resilient behaviors they are exhibiting and teaching them new coping strategies is a proactive approach that the students can use to help them rebound from difficult situations. The challenge approach suggests that a person has strengths and capabilities. The damage approach suggests that a person is woefully damaged and is a victim of circumstances. People who have experienced great difficulties in life may emerge from them stronger and more self-aware, or they may succumb and accept the victim identity. As educators, it is our job to make sure that youths know their strengths and make them part of their self-image so that they have an internal locus of control and perceive that they can influence things that affect them.

Try This Out With All Ages

There is no reason to wait until we are faced with a very bad situation to begin naming what kids are doing right, giving them that gift. Anytime you see a child doing something like holding a door or picking up another's pen, instead of saying, "Nice job," you could say, "You are a very considerate person for doing that." Or, when a child struggles to learn fractions, instead of saying, "Nice work," you could say, "You stuck with this even when you wanted to quit. You have such courage." Or "I can see how determined you are to learn this. Thank you for your effort." Kids need these specific words to really understand what they are doing and who they are. Having these words may not always make them do better in school, but they will certainly help them do better in life, which is, after all, our primary objective as educators.

The core of resiliency is relationship. Children and adolescents are placed in our care for up to 13 years. Whether we mean to or not, we will develop relationships with them. The quality of those relationships is, in large proportion, up to us. Most youths want adult approval and want respect. In a different era, teachers were often warned not to smile before Thanksgiving! The sad truth is that some still adhere to this rule. The days when students cooperated with and deferred to teachers just because they were the ones in the front of the room are long over. A new approach is needed.

One way to build relationship and show respect is to see children and adolescents for the people they are outside the classroom. If we wish to interact with students in genuine ways, we need to know who they are, what they can do, what they hope to be able to do, and what they believe. All we have to do is ask, listen, and observe.

Try This Out With All Ages

■ One way to begin forming relationships is to make a concerted effort to find something positive about each student and point that out with honesty and sincerity. These positives may be related to social interactions, dress, academics, athletics, or any number of things. For example, a student may arrive in school with a new hairstyle. Noticing it and complimenting it is a good way to begin. Another student may have scored a goal in soccer the night before. Mention it to the student individually, so that it is clear you are making the effort to connect. Believe me, the students will be glad you noticed—even if they act as if they aren't. Even though many students may not have had positive experiences with adults before, they appreciate being noticed.

■ Be persistent. Make the decision to remain in this for the long haul. Many long-lasting relationships have begun because a caring adult made an initial gesture of friendliness. A counselor told me that she recently attended a former student's wedding. They both laughed when they recalled the first day they met in his sixth-grade year. His angry, defiant response to her attempt to be friendly didn't stop her. She was persistently friendly, looked for opportunities to connect, and eventually a relationship began that even now shows no signs of ending. Let that be you. Be persistent with your students.

■ Laugh with students; share your thoughts and experiences. The simplicity of this approach is deceiving and may be a little frightening for teachers who do not want to lose classroom control. Don't confuse being genuine with being a pushover. Kids want and need clear boundaries and expectations. If students are not used to interacting with their educators on a more genuine level, they may not know how to react at first. It may take time and patience to build trust. Once students know that you are sincere, however, relationships will build.

Box 1.3

COMPARISON OF TWO RESILIENCY MODELS:
HENDERSON AND MILSTEIN'S AND
THE WOLINS'

HENDERSON AND MILSTEIN

What They Did. Synthesized research of Rutter, Werner and Smith, Garmezy, and many others. Developed useful models focusing on both the personal and environmental conditions that would lead to the development of competent adults.

Content. Personal characteristics of resilient people are

- Ability to elicit positive response
- Easy temperament
- Empathy or caring
- Communication skills
- Sense of humor
- Autonomy or self-efficacy
- Problem-solving skills
- Sense of purpose or future
- Environmental conditions in the home, school, and community that promote resiliency
- High expectations
- Caring and support
- Opportunities to participate

When To Use. This model gives guidance regarding the establishment of youth programs, creation of school climate, or improvement of personal lives.

(continued)

Box 1.3 Continued

Attributes of This Model

- Focuses heavily on the positive
- Gives hope to educators concerned for kids from high-risk environments
- Inspires creativity in adults who create environments
- Doesn't negate risk or pain, but doesn't focus on it

THE WOLINS

What They Did. Researched and identified behaviors in their clients that were evidence of resilience. Identified and defined seven resiliencies.

Content. Damage model versus Challenge model. Rather than focusing on peoples' weaknesses and their damage, resiliency-based therapy focuses on finding people's strengths by acknowledging their pain and reframing their experiences and their coping strategies, which become lifelong assets.

Seven Resiliencies

- Insight
- Independence
- Relationships
- Initiative
- Creativity
- Humor
- Morality

Box 1.3 Continued

When To Use. This model is useful in counseling but can also be useful in any caring interaction between two people. The listener can assist the talker in seeing how her or his actions reveal strength and ability to survive in spite of adversity.

Attributes of This Model

- Acknowledges pain and reframes it

- Acknowledges that a person may be very resilient in one area of his or her life and still have significant problems in another

- Offers people's actions to them in a way that they can use to create skills for future use

SOURCE: Benard, 1991; Henderson and Milstein, 1996; Wolin and Wolin, 1993.

Models Compared

In Box 1.3, the models of Henderson and Milstein, and of the Wolinses are briefly summarized and compared.

As the box shows, each model has its own usefulness. Henderson and Milstein's model is most useful in creating environments that foster resiliency but can also help to plan strategies for identified students. The Wolins' model is most useful in one-on-one interactions. These can be in counseling situations and in parent-child or educator-child interactions.

OVERVIEW OF ASSET BUILDING

A similar movement, asset building, has existed since 1989. The Search Institute, under the direction of Peter Benson, has been assisting communities with the concept of building assets in youths. There are striking similarities between resiliency theory and asset theory, and the two are very complementary. Search Institute (1997) has identified 40 assets that kids need to help them grow into healthy, competent adults. These assets are both internal and external, and fall into eight categories (see Figure 1.5).

Where Did You Get Your Assets?

Just as resiliency research indicates, asset theory states that some people may be born with more personal assets than others. In addition, Search (1997) asserts that adult-created environments and experiences are the primary builders of assets in our youths. The asset-building approach postulates that the more assets children have, the less likely they are to engage in risk-taking behavior.

One way to really grasp the importance of these assets is to spend a few minutes thinking about how you acquired them in your own adolescence. Look over the list of 40 assets (Figure 1.5) and their definitions one by one and, if you feel you had that asset as an adolescent, try to remember who or what helped you to have it. Who influenced you? Which adults in your life had a positive impact on you? What was your neighborhood like? Which people or organizations stand out for you? Which teachers believed in you? What messages did you receive from family or church, mosque, or synagogue about values? Did you hear values or see values? In other words, did you grow up hearing, "Do as I say, not as I do"? What were your family and extended family like? Was an organization such as Scouts a part of your life?

I have many friends who did not grow up in the best family circumstances. Very often, a neighbor or friend's mother became their surrogate parent. Through the caring and support of these people, my friends were able to acquire assets that assisted in their development. Sometimes, organizations or programs filled the parental gap. Boys & Girls Clubs of America are an example of an organization that provides the structure, consistency, and boundaries that many homes lack. Assets can come from many sources, both organizational and individual. A caring adult can make a huge difference in the life of a child.

Figure 1.5   40 Developmental Assets

ASSET TYPE		ASSET NAME	DEFINITIONS
EXTERNAL ASSETS	SUPPORT	1. Family support 2. Positive family communication 3. Other adult relationships 4. Caring neighborhood 5. Caring school climate 6. Parent involvement in schooling	Family life provides high levels of love and support Parents and child communicate positively; child is willing to seek parents advice and counsel Child receives support from three or more non-parent adults Child experiences caring neighbors School provides a caring, encouraging environment Parents are actively involved in helping child succeed in school
	EMPOWERMENT	7. Community values youth 8. Youth given useful roles 9. Community service 10. Safety	Child perceives that community adults value youth Youth are given useful roles in community life Child gives one hour or more per week to serving in one's community Child feels safe in home, school and neighborhood
	BOUNDARIES AND EXPECTATIONS	11. Family boundaries 12. School boundaries 13. Neighborhood boundaries 14. Adult role models 15. Positive peer influence 16. High expectations	Family has clear rules and consequences and monitors whereabouts School provides clear rules and consequences Neighbors would report undesirable behavior to family Parent(s) and other adults model prosocial behavior Child's best friends model responsible behavior Both parents and teachers press child to achieve
	TIME	17. Creative activities 18. Youth programs 19. Religious community 20. Time at home	Involved three or more hours per week in lessons or practice in music, theater, or other arts Involved three hours or more per week in sports, clubs, or organizations at school and/or in community organizations Involved one or more hours per week Out with friends "with nothing special to do" two or fewer nights per week
INTERNAL ASSETS	EDUCATIONAL COMMITMENT	21. Achievement motivation 22. School engagement 23. Homework 24. Bonding to school 25. Reading for pleasure	Child is motivated to do well in school Child is actively engaged in learning Child reports one or more hours of homework per day Child cares about her/his school Child reads for pleasure three or more hours per week
	VALUES	26. Caring 27. Equality and social justice 28. Integrity 29. Honesty 30. Responsibility 31. Restraint	Child places high value on helping other people Child places high value on promoting equality and reducing hunger and poverty Child acts on convictions, stands up for her or his beliefs Child "tells the truth even when it is not easy" Child accepts and takes personal responsibility Child believes it is important not to be sexually active or to use alcohol or other drugs
	SOCIAL COMPETENCIES	32. Planning and decision making 33. Interpersonal competence 34. Cultural competence 35. Resistance skills 36. Peaceful conflict resolution	Child has skill to plan ahead and make choices Child has empathy, sensitivity, and friendship skills Child has knowledge of and comfort with people of different racial backgrounds Child can resist negative peer pressure Child seeks to resolve conflict nonviolently
	POSITIVE IDENTITY	37. Personal control 38. Self-esteem 39. Sense of purpose 40. Positive view of personal future	Child feels she/he has control over "things that happen to me" Child reports high self-esteem Child reports "my life has a purpose" Child is optimistic about his/her personal future

© Search Institute, 700 South 3rd Street, Minneapolis, MN 55415, 612-376-8955

SOURCE: Reprinted with permission of Search Institute, *The Asset Approach: Giving Kids What They Need to Succeed.* Minneapolis, MN: Search Institute. © Search Institute, 1997. www.search-institute.org

As you think about your own youth and your acquisition of assets, two things may happen. First, you may realize that in your youth, you did not have all the assets or even half of them. You may wonder why you are doing so well in spite of it. You may begin to understand that you have innate internal assets. In addition, people may acquire assets throughout life and, no doubt, you are still building them through new experiences. Second, you may realize the debt you owe someone, or many people and experiences, for doing all they did so that you could grow into who you are. People in their 40s and 50s may realize how life has changed significantly over the past 30 years and see why many of today's youths are floundering. The supports that were once present in our neighborhoods and communities are no longer there for many children.

In 1996 to 1997, the Search Institute surveyed almost 100,000 students in Grades 6 to 12 in 213 towns and cities nationwide to determine how many assets these youths had. The results showed that the students had an average of 18 assets each. Older students seemed to have fewer assets than younger students; and boys had fewer assets than girls (Search Institute, 1997). Since youths rely on adults to create the environments that will help them acquire assets, the family, school, and community are keys to enhancing youths' ability to grow into competent adults. Kids today cannot do this alone any more than we did.

The survey that the Search Institute would conduct in a community that requests it measures the assets present in a community of youths. The utility of the survey is that it suggests solutions. For example, if the survey reveals that a great number of young people are unsupervised in the after-school hours, it would make sense to create programs for students after school. If the survey were to reveal that few young people are engaged in their communities in positive ways, then it would make sense for businesses and other organizations to create volunteer opportunities for kids. The asset model seeks to mobilize communities to create the support necessary for kids to acquire as many assets as possible. It relies on adults to mobilize themselves in order to create the ideal environment for kids and, like the resiliency model, it focuses heavily on the building of relationships with youths.

Using the Asset Approach to Understand Young People

One of the students in my graduate class did an interesting project. He was working with a group of five high-risk boys in an urban middle school. They were all in the group because of behavior or attitude problems. He asked them to take the brief asset checklist in Figure 1.6.

The exercise, which should not be confused with a valid survey, revealed some very important information. While all the boys varied in their responses somewhat, all five answered no to the following statements:

My neighbors encourage and support me.

My school provides a caring, encouraging environment.

I feel valued by adults in my community.

I am given useful roles in my community.

I serve in the community 1 hour or more each week.

I care about my school.

I read for pleasure 3 or more hours each week.

I believe it is important not to be sexually active or to use alcohol or drugs.

I believe I have control over many things that happen to me.

Adults who wish to build assets in youths can get quite a bit of useful information and direction from the answers to these questions. Is it any wonder that these youths were acting out? Is it any wonder that they felt so disenfranchised? Their community and school surely could do a better job of

Figure 1.6   An Asset Checklist

Many people find it helpful to use a simple checklist to reflect on the assets young people experience. This checklist simplifies the asset list to help prompt conversation in families, organizations, and communities.

○ 1. I receive high levels of love and support from family members.

○ 2. I can go to my parent(s) or guardian(s) for advice and support and have frequent, in-depth conversations with them.

○ 3. I know some nonparent adults I can go to for advice and support.

○ 4. My neighbors encourage and support me.

○ 5. My school provides a caring, encouraging environment.

○ 6. My parent(s) or guardian(s) help me succeed in school.

○ 7. I feel valued by adults in my community.

○ 8. I am given useful roles in my community.

○ 9. I serve in the community one hour or more each week.

○ 10. I feel safe at home, at school, and in the neighborhood.

○ 11. My family sets standards for appropriate conduct and monitors my whereabouts.

○ 12. My school has clear rules and consequences for behavior.

○ 13. Neighbors take responsibility for monitoring my behavior.

○ 14. Parent(s) and other adults model positive, responsible behavior.

○ 15. My best friends model responsible behavior.

○ 16. My parent(s)/guardian(s) and teachers encourage me to do well.

○ 17. I spend three hours or more each week in lessons or practice in music, theater, or other arts.

○ 18. I spend three or more hours each week in school or community sports, clubs, or organizations.

○ 19. I spend one hour or more each week in religious services or participating in spiritual activities.

○ 20. I go out with friends "with nothing special to do" two or fewer nights each week.

○ 21. I want to do well in school.

○ 22. I am actively engaged in learning.

○ 23. I do an hour or more of homework each school day.

○ 24. I care about my school.

○ 25. I read for pleasure three or more hours each week.

○ 26. I believe it is really important to help other people.

○ 27. I want to help promote equality and reduce world poverty and hunger.

○ 28. I can stand up for what I believe.

○ 29. I tell the truth even when it's not easy.

○ 30. I can accept and take personal responsibility.

○ 31. I believe it is important not to be sexually active or to use alcohol or other drugs.

○ 32. I am good at planning ahead and making decisions.

○ 33. I am good at making and keeping friends.

○ 34. I know and am comfortable with people of different cultural/racial/ethnic backgrounds.

○ 35. I can resist negative peer pressure and dangerous situations.

○ 36. I try to resolve conflict nonviolently.

○ 37. I believe I have control over many things that happen to me.

○ 38. I feel good about myself.

○ 39. I believe my life has a purpose.

○ 40. I am optimistic about my future.

SOURCE: Reprinted with permission of Search Institute, *The Asset Approach: Giving Kids What They Need to Succeed.* Minneapolis, MN: Search Institute. © Search Institute, 1997. www.search-institute.org

NOTE: This checklist is neither intended nor appropriate as a scientific or accurate measurement of developmental assets.

engaging them in useful activities, which would build their assets and prepare them for their futures. I am reminded of a quote by Sarason (1990) which says,

> When one has no stake in the way things are, when one's needs or opinions are provided no forum, when one sees oneself as the object of unilateral actions, it takes no particular wisdom to suggest that one would rather be elsewhere. (p. 89)

I think these boys would agree. With the information from this checklist, caring adults could immediately begin to remedy this sad situation. It is clear that these young men need adult connection. They need to feel useful and necessary to the operation of their school and their communities. Surely, a creative adult could create opportunities for these young people to contribute in meaningful ways. By having a simple conversation, it would be possible to find out about their interests and skills. These may not be academic, but still could be very useful, for example, in assisting younger children to learn the basics of basketball or another sport. Determining their interests and then offering them ways to share their skills and knowledge can engage students. Having opportunities to contribute would certainly communicate to them that school is a caring and supportive place. This is not extremely complicated to do, but it does take motivation and effort. More important, it takes adults who truly believe that each child has talents and resources to share and abilities to be nurtured. In other words, it takes adults who possess the resiliency attitude.

Youths like the ones who filled out this checklist have been born into less than ideal circumstances. Like the dandelions that landed on blacktopped parking lots, they may not experience safety and nurturing in their communities. Their families may rely heavily on the schools to provide asset-building environments and experiences for them. Youths need adults in schools more than ever to do their parts before it is too late. Since the nurturing neighborhoods where adults looked out for all kids are less likely to exist, due to increased mobility or economic distress, youths often look for and find a social connection among themselves. This may lead to their taking life-compromising chances for fun and to relieve boredom. Others may join gangs where protection and belonging is offered in exchange for undying loyalty, which often translates into dying for loyalty. We cannot let this happen. When teachers and other educators pay attention to youths as individuals and inspire hope in their futures, they have other options for connection. I believe that hope in a bright future provides a reason to abide by rules, to study, and to dream of possibilities.

Socioeconomics Are Not the Issue

In our suburbs, many youths today have never been so affluent, and yet many have never been so asset poor. It would be easy to assume that those who are materially rich would also be asset rich. This, however, is not always the case. How can this be? The answer is simple. As we learned from the research synthesized by Benard (1991), building relationships is the key to success with youths. As many families in our society have become more and more focused on attaining and sustaining prosperity, they have lost focus on developing and maintaining sound relationships with their children. As an example, some families who have kids involved in a wide variety of outside activities have forfeited the family dinner. Likewise, some parents who are overinvolved in careers or social activities have turned their attention away from making the home a safe refuge. Many families do not worship on a regular basis. Stress abounds as everyone struggles to maintain the level of income and social involvement that has become equated with success. The Search Institute's asset approach is a very simple way to begin to think of ways to remedy situations described above.

As we move through this book, it will become apparent how good educational practice builds assets and, therefore, resiliency in students. You will begin to see what part you, as an educator, may play in helping kids develop assets. For example, educational commitment can be nurtured when teachers make sure that everything taught in the classroom is rich, interesting, and meaningful to all students. Relate what students are learning to their lives so they can see why it is meaningful. In Chapter 3, we will see how attending to multiple intelligences and learning styles can help students engage in their learning. In order to provide support, educators might see to it that the classroom and total school environment communicate to students that they are safe, respected, and valued. As we move through this book, there will be many tips for doing these things. Coincidentally, the values described are the very ones encouraged by the character education movement, which we will learn more about in Chapter 2. Students who possess these values also possess assets. The asset-building movement encourages all adults in a community to get involved in building assets in their youth. The school environment is ripe with opportunities to build assets in students.

Resiliency and asset building are very similar movements. Kids become resilient when adults create the environments, big or small, in which kids can build skills and thrive. Asset building encourages mobilizing schools, families, and communities to create broad change where kids are embraced and valued. However, kids also develop assets when Henderson and Milstein's (1996) wheel is put into action. These are compatible models that can be incorporated simultaneously.

Try Asking Yourself These Questions

As we have discussed, the resiliency approach starts with changing our mind-sets. Once our thinking changes, our actions follow. As teachers and other educators reflect on the atmospheres they create in their classrooms and offices, they might ask themselves wheel-related questions. These questions might even be discussed among trusted colleagues.

Do I Provide Care and Support? Most important, do I communicate in words and actions that I truly care about, respect, and support my students? There is ample research to support the notion that students will do almost anything for teachers whom they like and who they believe like them. Nel Noddings said, "It is obvious that children will work harder and do things—even odd things like adding fractions—for people they love and trust" (cited in Benard, 1991, p. 10).

Do I Set and Communicate High Expectations? Do I really believe that all students can succeed, and do I provide the necessary support for that to happen? Do I address learning styles, and do I consider different intelligences in my teaching? What have I planned for the kids who need to touch and feel and move? Is there an opportunity for individual children to demonstrate what they are good at? Do I gladly make accommodations for different styles and personalities?

Do I Provide Opportunities for Meaningful Participation? What opportunities can I create for my students to contribute to the smooth operation of the classroom or school building? What jobs can be delegated to students? What roles and responsibilities can the students assume? Can students be responsible for keeping books on shelves or caring for animals? Could they take turns teaching each other something new that reflects their outside school interests? Can high school students tutor younger ones?

Do I Increase Prosocial Bonding? How can I promote prosocial bonding? Do I use cooperative learning strategies? Do I connect students in ways that help them get to know one another? Do I seek to break up cliques and to involve everyone in ways that show their strengths? Do I give respect and expect it from others?

Do I Set Clear, Consistent Boundaries? Do we, as a class or school community, develop clear rules and expectations? Are there logical consequences and are they enforced consistently and fairly? Are all teachers and staff on the same page with rules?

Do I Teach Life Skills? Am I teaching life skills that help students make decisions or resolve conflicts? Do my students get to practice making decisions? Can they choose from a variety of topics for projects? Are there options for them to demonstrate their knowledge? How will I teach them to work as a team member? Do I model courtesy and politeness as well as expect it from students?

Answering the Questions. In later chapters, more specific strategies will be offered, which will help us answer these questions. Educators who thoughtfully consider these questions, and intentionally create the environments in which they and their students will spend an entire year, find that the effort is well worth it. The time and energy used in setting the stage for classroom life pays dividends as the year progresses. There will be less time spent on conflict and behavior problems and more left for academics.

SUMMARY

Do you remember that clown punching bag that was popular for so many years? It was about 3 feet tall, and when a child punched it, it popped right back up again. In order to understand resiliency, it is helpful to remember why the clown was able to pop back up. It is because the clown is weighted at the bottom. It is connected, or grounded, so that even when it gets knocked down, it can roll with the punches, so to speak. In a very real sense, this is why resilient people are resilient. They are connected to others in positive ways, and they are grounded with the weight of their own assets so that when they take a hit from life, they do not stay down for long.

As we look at each educational megatrend in this book, the connection to building resiliency will become clear.

It is often a relief for school staff to develop this understanding—resiliency building for students in schools is the foundation of excellent education as that concept has been defined in the last decade, and excellent education will produce resiliency building. (Henderson & Milstein, 1996, p. 31)

2

Character Education and Building Resilience

Everything a school does teaches values—including the way teachers and other adults treat students, the way the principal treats teachers, the way the school treats parents, and the way students are allowed to treat school staff and each other.

—Thomas Lickona (1991, p. 20)

B uilding resiliency is not done through one program or a specific curriculum. People who create environments—in which children live and learn—foster resiliency (or not) through their attitudes toward youths, their ability to build relationships with them, and through the use of key strategies. This is a process during which adults interact with children to nurture their innate seeds of resiliency. Now, reread these sentences and try substituting the word *character* for *resiliency*. The sentences

45

still make perfect sense. Just as with resiliency, children most often develop character (or not) because of the quality of their interactions with the significant adults in their immediate environments.

For many reasons, the character education movement is perceived as something new. It isn't. It only seems new because the name did not exist before the 1990s. Educating students' characters was considered by the founders of our educational system to be an essential aspect of a child's education. Thomas Jefferson believed that only if people had moral law within themselves could a free government survive (Lickona, 1991). Our first schools were expected to make people smart and make them good. Teachers were expected to model and teach correct behavior. While not specifically titled character education, this concept was the norm for many years. Over time, we moved away from teaching character, or values, in our schools for many reasons, one of which was the fear that we would offend or be politically incorrect. Perhaps, now we have come full circle, because the well is running dry, and we are beginning to miss the water. What was once considered to be an integral part of a child's education is now being reinstituted in response to multiple crises which highlight the apparent lack of character in our children. As is often the case, the focus is on the children rather than on the adults and the adult-created environments within which children function on a daily basis. How can we expect youths to escape the impact of adults and adult-driven systems, such as schools, organized sports, the Internet, entertainment, or the media? How can we expect them to change if we and our systems do not?

As with resiliency, the home, school, and community, ideally, ought to be the arenas for character-building efforts. As we know, educators can directly influence only their own actions within the school setting. Even so, we cannot be reminded too often that resiliency literature underscores the immense potential for educators within schools to positively influence kids in spite of their other circumstances.

Character Education Lost

If character was once implied in the term *education*, what happened to change all that? What follows is a very brief account of where we were and how we got to where we are. For many years, the children of this country were educated in one-room schoolhouses. When someone is trying to pictorially represent a school, the image used is the one-room schoolhouse with a bell in the steeple. This image is rooted in our imaginations. It is where it all began. As history progressed, the Industrial Revolution drastically changed this scene. People flocked to the cities for jobs, immigrants arrived continuously, and population boomed. Bigger schools were needed to meet the needs of this country's youths. Later, as child labor laws sent droves of children from factories to the schools' doorsteps, and compulsory attendance laws were passed, schools stretched and grew. One-room schoolhouses, fixtures of early settlements and of agricultural and rural life, were no longer sufficient. Larger schools were built, and a new system was developed to address the growing need for educating the masses.

A logical solution to the student boom was to group children by age rather than by readiness or achievement. All 5-year-olds were in one grade, all 6-year-olds were in the next, and so on. Cut-off dates were established so that everyone knew what grade a child ought to be in. It no longer seemed to matter that some 5-year-olds were not ready for school at all, while some were ready for second grade. Schools seemed to lose focus on the unique aspects of each child in order to meet the needs of the larger majority. It was the democratic way, and, apparently, there seemed to be no other choice. The movement reflected the best thinking of the time. Now, as we continue to discover more about how brains learn and how children develop, it becomes painfully apparent that we lost a great deal when we moved away from the one-room schoolhouse concept. In the new system that remains with us today, children are no longer grouped by readiness but, rather, by age, with a few exceptions for accelerated or delayed children. As the size of our schools increased, attention to individuality decreased. With more attention being devoted to managing the masses, teachers' opportunities to have the kind of relationships with their students that help to build character diminished.

Many one-room schoolhouses were character-building and resiliency-building structures with the basics built right in. In our current system, we are working hard to incorporate these elements into our schools. One-room schoolhouses already were multiaged classrooms. Students and teachers stayed together for many years, as one teacher taught every child rather than a specific grade. Schools now call this strategy looping. The opportunities for interage connections were many, as older students helped younger ones and children learned at their own pace. These environments were conducive to building resiliency and character, especially because of the opportunities to develop individual relationships. The child-centered attributes of the one-room schoolhouse were sacrificed for systematic convenience.

Lickona (1991) informs us that these and many other forces led to the decline of character education. In the 1920s, two empirical psychologist researchers, Hartshorne and May, found no evidence that an internal state called *character* existed (Lickona, 1991). Their theory, called the doctrine of specificity, stated that the behavior of people is highly variable and not dependent on an internal state of character. Thus began a movement away from character education that remained with us through the next few, war-torn decades. Making value judgments fell out of favor, and people were reluctant to say something was right or wrong, good or bad. Being judgmental was considered unattractive and even socially risky (Lickona, 1991).

According to Lickona, during the 1960s and 1970s, many felt that personal freedom was more important than responsibility and commitment. As more people focused on their personal needs and self-fulfillment, many abandoned the notion of remaining in jobs or relationships if they became uncomfortable or dissatisfying. As a result, people became more mobile.

In addition, the divorce rate rose continually, and more children have grown up experiencing the effects of divorce than ever before. As the family's stability and influence has declined, drug use, violence, pregnancy, and HIV/AIDS have increased (Lickona, 1991).

Children Need Adults More Than Ever

In the absence of clearly communicated values and standards, children will develop their own. In such instances, they are easy prey for unscrupulous adults wanting to exploit them. Music stars, movie and television stars, or athletes become role models rather than educators, parents, grandparents, aunts and uncles. In today's world, many youths are developing their own cultures because adults have given them so little direction. Many parents are so busy providing expensive things for themselves and their children that they have neglected to provide some things for them that are priceless: parental time and guidance.

Neighbors, and even some educators in the school setting, who once corrected the misbehavior of children are often reluctant to do so because parents may view this as interference rather than assistance. Kids who arrive home in the afternoon long before their parents do often spend many hours on the computer, specifically the Internet. In my discussions with other parents, most with minimal computer skills, it is clear that many are unaware of what their children are doing on the Internet. They often have an idea of the potential for harm that exists without proper supervision but usually rely on verbal instructions to avoid dangerous situations and hope for the best. Is it any surprise that formalized character education is returning in direct response to these trends? The bothersome aspect, I believe, is that this movement is almost entirely focused on improving children's character rather than on the behavior and character of the adults who care for them.

Some states have legislated that schools will teach character education as part of their curriculum. While this may seem to be a good idea, the belief that character education can be *taught* is troublesome, to say the least. This language reflects a belief that character education is a requirement that could be met by teaching children a specific number of lessons on topics such as respect or responsibility. Adults are often not mentioned in the effort at all. If we are not careful, we will go down the same pot-holed road that drug prevention once went down. Character education will be perceived as a school event. The result will be that adults who are responsible for creating environments and modeling appropriate behavior will not accept their responsibility. In their minds, children will have good character because their curriculum provided 15 lessons in the seventh grade, with some booster lessons later on. Unless adults accept responsibility for creating positive environments and modeling the character traits they wish children to have, all the lessons in the world will do no good. Character education is a lifelong process that has *relationship* at its core. If parents, educators, and other adults spend time building relationships with youths, then youths will have character.

WHAT IS CHARACTER EDUCATION?

Lickona breaks character education into three main areas: moral knowing, moral feeling, and moral action. In other words, it involves the head, the heart, and the hands. Children need to *know* what to do, need to *want* to do it, and need to be *motivated to action*. Lickona's views of these three aspects of character education are summarized below.[1]

Moral Knowing: The Head

1. **Moral awareness**. This is the ability to know when a judgment on an issue must be made. If children are asked to cheat on a test, will they ask themselves, "Is this right to do?"

2. **Knowing moral values**. This means that children understand what respect and responsibility look like. If children are faced with the opportunity to deface property, will they know how to apply the concept?

3. **Perspective taking**. This means being able to see the perspective of others. Will a child be able to understand why another student acts in a certain way?

4. **Moral reasoning**. Children need to know what is moral and why. For example, keeping a promise is something that needs to be taken seriously because it indicates that we have integrity and can be trusted.

5. **Decision making**. Children need to be able to think their way through a problem. If children are faced with joining in on teasing another child, will they be able to make a decision that reflects the value of empathy?

6. **Self-knowledge**. It is important for young people to be able to review their behavior and evaluate it. Can children reflect on their behavior and decide if they would do things differently next time? This ensures that learning has taken place.

Moral Feeling: The Heart

1. **Conscience**. A child must first know what is right and then feel obligated to do what is right. For example, not cheating even when tempted because it is wrong.

2. **Self-esteem**. It is important that youths value themselves so that they may value others. When we like ourselves, we do not have to make others look or feel small.

3. **Empathy**. This is being able to identify with the feelings or situations of others: for example, knowing how it feels to be the new kid in school, or how it feels to lose a parent. (Another author who has written about the emotional growth of children, Goleman [1995], relates

that children are innately empathetic but can lose this attribute if it is not nurtured.)

4. **Loving the good**. This means that children take plea-sure in doing good. It involves training the heart as well as the mind. Young people are quick to understand that to give is to receive. Most are eager to help when given the opportunity.

5. **Self-control**. It is not easy being good or ethical when we don't want to be. Self-control means restraining our desires because it is the right thing to do: for example, not butting in line but waiting our turn.

6. **Humility**. This means being open to the truth and being willing to correct misbehavior.

Moral Action: The Hands

1. **Competence.** This means having the necessary skills to turn moral judgment into action: for example, teaching children the skills necessary to solve conflict.

2. **Will.** Children must mobilize the moral energy to do what they think they should: for example, resisting temptation or standing up for themselves and others.

3. **Habit.** When children and young adults have character, they do the right thing by force of habit.

Character Education Can Be Controversial

There have been many critics of character education, including Kohn (1997), an educator, author and lecturer, who believes that character education can be seen in two ways. The broad view, which Kohn prefers, is that character education is anything that schools do to try to help children grow into good people. The narrow view is a type of moral training that reflects particular values as well as assumptions about the nature of children and how they learn. He believes that many proponents of the character education movement have a dark view of children that implies that children do not have intrinsic goodness but must be taught to be good; that they are consumers of our efforts rather than participants in a process. In some character education efforts, where attention is only on the character or behavior of the youths, and where words like *respect* and *responsibility* are merely pasted on walls, this is a very valid criticism. Kohn writes,

> More than specific practices that might be added, subtracted, or changed, a program to help children grow into good people begins with a commitment to change the way classrooms and schools are structured—and this brings us back to the idea of transcending a fix-the-kid approach. (p. 437)

In Lickona's (1998, p. 454) response to Kohn's (1997, p. 437) criticisms of character education, he agrees that the broad, or comprehensive, approach is best. Both cite the Child Development Project, which was designed, implemented, and researched by the Developmental Studies Center in Oakland, California, as an example of a program that is committed to changing the culture of a school.

Adults too often think that by naming a value of the month and focusing visuals and activities for children around it, their jobs are done. This simplistic view of character education is dangerous because it does not acknowledge that educators and other adults are ultimately responsible for creating character-building environments every day. In the narrow view, the focus remains on the children and getting them to be more respectful or courteous, regardless of the daily environments in which they must function. If children are not learning in environments where their unique needs are respected, and if they are not interacting with the knowledge that they are safe from ridicule or abuse, other efforts toward character development will be entirely wasted.

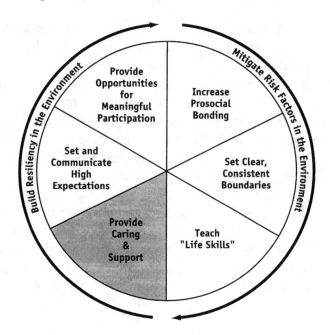

Character education is better when it is lived than when it is taught. As the saying goes, children do what we do, not what we say. When adults create the situations in which character building is natural, children internalize it. It is not perceived as something extra but, rather, something essential. When students are immersed in character-building schools, they are more likely to emerge with character. It is indeed unfortunate that we must make character education an obvious activity when character should be developed naturally over time with adults leading the way.

WORKING THE WHEEL

As we reflect on the climate of our schools and, more specifically, the environments of our classrooms and offices, it is helpful to look at each segment of the resiliency wheel and determine the degree to which we incorporate the strategies into our daily routines. If we want to build character and resilience, the wheel shows us the way. Couple this with a resiliency attitude that considers all children to be potential resources, and we are in business. Many tired educators ask, "How can I teach character education when I have so many other things to do?" The answer is simple: Don't teach it, live it.

As you know, the resiliency wheel is divided into six segments, each representing a strategy for building resilience. The more parts of the wheel that you include in all that you do, the more likely you will be to get the results you want. We will now look at each segment of the wheel and focus on strategies for building character. Competent educators may already be doing wonderful things and not even realize that they are building character and resiliency. That is terrific, and I believe that with this new knowledge, you will be even more deliberate about what you do.

Provide Caring and Support

This segment of the wheel is the most important. Students who believe that their teachers, principals, counselors, and other school staff members truly like them and care about them are generally happier and more motivated to do well. Children develop sound character when they experience adults modeling caring, honesty, respect, responsibility, courage, and empathy.

Try This Out With All Ages

- Find out when your students' birthdays are and acknowledge them, even if it is nothing more than saying "Happy birthday!" to a student at the beginning of class. Even high school students like it when people remember their birthdays.
- Send cards to students who will be out sick for more than a day or two. Better yet, phone and see how the student is doing. With permission, tell other students if a classmate is ill so that they may also show their concern with a card or a call.

- Make home visits whenever possible to get to know the students and their families. It is a great way to develop understanding and empathy for your students.
- Greet and welcome students at the door to your classroom. Call them by name and notice something positive about each one as they enter. Say good-bye in the same way. We do this for guests in our home. Why shouldn't we for our students?
- Show respect first, before you expect it to be returned. Let the kids know you like them. (If you don't like them, should you rethink your career?)
- Give students a few minutes in each class to share something about themselves or about something relevant to them to let them know that you know they have interests other than class material and that you are interested in them.
- Ask them their opinions about issues, and try to weave them into class content.
- Allow students to have choices. Let them choose from a variety of options when assigning work or assessing it.

Try This Out as an Entire School

- Create newcomers groups that pair established students with new students to ease the transition into the school community.
- Offer groups to assist students who are struggling with life issues such as divorce, death or loss, family problems, peer relationships, and so forth.
- Create drop-in rooms for students who are struggling with reintegrating into the school community from treatment for physical, mental, or substance abuse problems.
- Offer parent support groups for parents who would like to share strategies and get support during the difficult parenting years.

Set and Communicate High Expectations

This segment of the wheel is important because young people need to feel competent and capable. If parents and educators expect students to achieve, and provide the necessary support so that they will be successful, youths will almost always meet their expectations. Working hard and experiencing the feeling of accomplishment is character building. It is also self-esteem building because children develop an internal locus of control when they see that they are responsible for their own success. They learn to identify their strengths and use them to build new ones.

Try This Out With Elementary Students

- Help them to set personal goals, such as reading six new books in a semester. Teach them to keep track of progress with their own chart.
- Set a time with each of your students to assist them in setting a personal learning goal for the year. Check in every 2 weeks, individually, to see how progress is coming.
- Allow students to prepare their own portfolios of their work for parents' night.

Try This Out With Middle or Secondary Students

- Work with your students to set their class project goals together. During the process, discuss ways for them to build in the support necessary to be successful. For example, if a student's goal is to write a play by the end of the semester, help the student see what prior actions would be needed to be successful: reading sample plays, deciding on a comedy or tragedy, seeing a play, setting up a timeline, and so forth. Sometimes, students do not know what is entailed in meeting a lofty goal. As teachers, it is our job to encourage lofty goals and assist students in meeting them.

■ Allow students the opportunity to evaluate their performance whenever possible. Assist them in reviewing their actions and determining which were helpful and which ought to be changed. Communicate to students how important this learning is as it helps them to set new goals or adjust current ones. Instead of focusing on right and wrong answers, they will learn to appreciate the process of learning.

■ Let all students know that you are open to their ideas but that there are standards that they must meet. For example, let students choose a topic or a project based on their interest, but set the performance standards and help them to achieve them.

■ Consider inviting students to facilitate their own parent-teacher conferences.

Provide Opportunities for Meaningful Participation

This is my favorite part of the wheel because I have seen the transformation that occurs when students are offered the opportunity to do something that is perceived by others to be useful. Children and adolescents almost always jump at the chance to do something important, to contribute in some way. Activities can be created that will develop a desired character trait. For example, there is no better way to create empathy than to experience, even for a short time, what another experiences. And what better way to develop responsibility than to have an animal or plant dependent on you for survival?

Try This Out With All Ages

■ Collect clothing and other items for needy people or homeless shelters. Have children sort and package the things collected. Conversations during the process are great opportunities to discuss how the recipients live and feel.

■ Assign jobs and responsibilities that students can perform that contribute to the smooth running of the classroom, for example, collecting or passing out supplies, erasing blackboards, taking attendance, rewinding videos, watering plants, feeding animals. Students can be part of identifying jobs to be done and developing a rotating system so that each student has a turn at a job.

■ Arrange with local adult group homes for students to visit and interact with the elderly.

■ Allow students to assist with keeping school grounds attractive. Students can plant and care for gardens.

Try This Out With Middle or Secondary Students

■ Recruit students to offer assistance to younger students, academically, athletically, or socially. Have older students write and act out vignettes that model life skills, such as resisting negative peer pressure. Then have the older kids lead a discussion to process this with the younger students.

Increase Prosocial Bonding

Children develop the character traits of empathy and acceptance when they appreciate and understand one another. Anything educators can do to foster these traits among students will help them to bond to each other and to the school itself.

Try This Out With Elementary and Middle Levels

■ Create opportunities on a regular basis for students to share the unique aspects of their culture, traditions, or interests outside school. This promotes understanding of differences as well as identification of similarities. For example, as you facilitate conversations about holiday traditions, favorite meals, favorite TV shows or movies, sports, and so forth, students see that even though some students have different experiences from their own, there are also many things that they have in common.

■ Offer opportunities for students to share hobbies or interests with the entire class. Students might even teach others in the class something they know how to do, like origami. Maybe a student would like to present a card collection or talk about some other hobby. These activities would also meet the English and Language Arts standard for oral communication.

■ Use cooperative-learning strategies that require students to work as part of a group or team. Be sure to form groups carefully, and structure them so that no one is left out or allowed to coast while others do all the work.

■ Provide after-school activities that encourage students to meet one another. These do not have to be athletic activities. A counselor I know created an after-school Scrapbook Club for kids who are not interested in sports. Students bring pictures from home and work together at a table as they create their own individual scrapbooks. The conversations flow naturally as students ask questions about pictures, and everyone gets to talk about their lives outside of school. This is especially wonderful for shy students, because it is easier to talk when their hands are busy and other kids are looking at something besides them.

Set Clear, Consistent Boundaries

Students need, and often desire, clear and consistent boundaries. Without them, students lack the safety net that catches them before they get hurt. It is our job to create a net, if you will, that is flexible enough to allow students to learn from mistakes but strong enough to keep them from hitting the ground. I recently overheard my son's friend saying that he wished his science teacher would give a few detentions instead of just threatening to do so. Very few students would openly ask their teacher to enforce the rules, but most students expect that teachers will. Character is built when adults model the behaviors they expect students to have and offer logical consequences for occasions when students overstep the boundaries set forth by caring adults. Younger students, although they can help with this process, must rely more on adults to set boundaries and expectations. Older students respond better to a more democratic system where their ideas and needs are taken into account. Most educators I have talked to have found that students are much more willing to abide by and enforce rules that they have helped to create.

Try This Out With All Ages

■ Spend time at the beginning of the year facilitating a discussion on rules of behavior that would help the class run smoothly and ensure that everyone has the chance to learn. Once consensus is reached, have students record the rules and keep them in clear view so all can refer to them. In addition to helping students learn the concept of consensus, this activity blends nicely with the social studies standard having to do with citizenship.

■ Let parents know what the class's decision was by sending them a copy.

■ Enforce the rules consistently and fairly for all. As hard as it is sometimes to dish out the punishment, it does a disservice to students to set a rule and then overlook it. It takes energy to enforce rules, but it takes more energy to deal with the aftermath of ignoring them or enforcing them arbitrarily.

Teach Life Skills

Students, like all of us, usually learn best by experience. They need opportunities to practice life skills. In a safe, orderly classroom with a safety net ready to catch them, students can try out skills that will serve them long after school is over.

Try This Out With All Ages

■ Institute a program or protocol for resolving disputes. In elementary classrooms, it may be easier because students remain in the classroom most of the day. A special corner (in elementary school) or a room (in upper grades) where two students can go to sit with a teacher or trained peer mediator to talk out differences is a great way to prepare students for the inevitable conflicts of life.

■ Help students learn how to advocate for themselves, to speak up when they are cold or too warm, to ask for assistance.

■ Model the courtesy you wish to receive. Never assume that students know the rules of civility, because their homes may not be teaching them. Begin by making clear what you expect, and show them what it looks like. Remember, this is a skill that may take time to develop.

■ Use literature and social studies to reinforce character. Assist students in identifying specific character traits of story characters or historical figures and the behaviors that accompany them. Help them to apply the concepts to their own lives.

I believe that if children seem to be unruly, disenfranchised, hopeless, and apparently devoid of character, we can look to our adult-driven systems for the reasons. It is up to adults to reclaim our youths and help them to find the competent, capable people inside.

Our students need us to have high expectations, apply consequences that teach them when they make mistakes, and affirm them for who they are. They need us to not give up on them, especially when they are giving up on themselves. (Mendler, 2000, p. 65)

Tips for Getting Started

Now that character education is being promoted and, in some cases, mandated, many schools will be looking for ways to begin. We can learn a lot from those who have been working more deliberately on character education for a few years now. The Character Education Partnership (CEP) (1996) publishes actual school stories about getting started and maintaining momentum. After reading many of these scenarios, it is clear that each school is unique. The manner in which a school addresses character education depends on many factors. There is no one correct way to begin incorporating character education more deliberately into a school or district. The important thing is that school communities work together to create the environments and provide the experiences for their children that will assist them in forming solid characters.

SUMMARY

Educating for character was once an integral part of the educational process. For many reasons, modern education lost sight of this critical part of itself. The character education movement of the 1990s was resurrected in response to a perceived lack of civility and character displayed by our young students. Schools have begun instituting programs in an attempt to restore character in their students. Some have been successful, others have not. The key is that, in addition to focusing on students, school communities must address the character traits and behavior toward students of the adults who create the school environment. If they do not, little will come of their efforts.

Some say that children have lost their heroes. Some fear that young people have become cynical and that they don't believe in the things that their parents believed in, like the adage, "honesty is the best policy." Many young people have grown up hearing people say that good guys finish last. They have observed, and learned from, politicians who have publicly admitted criminal acts and suffered little repercussion. Stores are stocked with T-shirts that scream, "Winning isn't everything, it's the only thing!" Do we really think that kids are immune to these influences? We must remember that our students, who seem to lack character, are reflections of the role models that surround them in the home and community as well as the school. As educators, we can help students to recognize good character in themselves and in others. English literature and history are full of examples of people who took the high road even when it was the harder road to take. In addition to making sure the curriculum includes examples of good character, we can also provide children with opportunities to make contributions.

For generations, kids have had heroes. How can they believe in heroes if their parents and teachers no longer do? Maybe our heroes are right under our noses and not just on baseball fields and movie screens, or in the Senate or the White House. On September 11, 2001, every kid in America saw heroes in action. The police, firefighters, emergency workers, and citizens who gave their all to help total strangers were exhibiting character of the best kind. Kids noticed and wanted to do their part in kind. That is the power of role models.

Sometimes, character is acquired through experiences where we are put to the test and we pass. Let's not forget that it is also acquired when we are put to the test and we fail, but a caring, supportive adult is nearby ready to help us understand how to do better next time. The important idea is that character can best be developed when kids have adults who care enough to expect them to do their best and stick with them as they try. These include the adults who deliberately work the resiliency wheel.

NOTE

1. Lickona, T. (1991). *Educating for Character: How Our Schools Can Teach Respect and Responsibility*, pp. 53-63. Bantam Books. Used with permission.

3

Multiple Intelligences Theory and Building Resilience

What I argue against is the notion that there is only one way to learn how to read, only one way to learn how to compute, only one way to learn about biology. I think that such contentions are nonsense.

— Howard Gardner (cited in Checkley, 1997, p. 10)

MULTIPLE INTELLIGENCES AND RESILIENCY

What a waste of talent and potential if students emerge from our schools with little or no idea of the ways in which they are intelligent. Having this knowledge can only serve to make them more engaged in their futures, and having hope in a future is a hallmark of resiliency. As we know, four of the wheel's strategies for building resiliency are providing caring and support, having high expectations, providing opportunities for participation, and teaching life skills. Attending to multiple intelligences and learning styles is a part of all four of these strategies. Resilient youth are those who appreciate their own abilities because others, usually teachers and parents, have high expectations for them and provide the resources and support necessary to achieve their goals. They feel that they can contribute in meaningful ways to others and to their own learning because they experience that teachers and other educators recognize and support their unique intelligences. This is the ultimate in care and support. Those who know themselves well and are confident in their abilities possess the most important life skills of all. To be really seen by a teacher is a true gift to a student. To have someone recognize your talents and personality traits, acknowledge and respect them, and actually teach in the way that you learn best would be a joyful experience for any child.

I wonder how many students have knocked on their counselors' doors to complain that a certain teacher hates them, or that they hate a teacher. Or how many students have complained that the teacher goes too fast, too slow, talks in riddles, makes no sense, calls on them when their hands aren't up, and isn't fair? Nurses know too well how many little folks come to school with tummy aches every day. No doubt the number is enormous. I would be willing to bet that many of these complaints have a common denominator: failure to thrive in school. No kindergarten student enters school intending to fail or to become a problem. Children are no different from adults in their desire to do well and to be successful at tasks that others deem important. Unsuccessful students often do not understand why they are unsuccessful, especially if they are trying. Some students reason that it must be the teacher's fault and take out their frustrations in disruptive ways. Some become anxious and take it out on themselves, often becoming physically ill. In the worst scenarios, unsuccessful students conclude that they are simply stupid and stop trying in order to avoid more failure. They may invent ways to avoid being seen as unintelligent, all the while trying to assure others that they really don't value school success. They may turn into clowns or bullies. Only very resilient students with strong adult support, or incredible internal strength, seem to have the fortitude to keep plugging away at schoolwork when school has not been a place to experience success.

Learning Styles Are Very Important

In a study conducted of at-risk learners, it was learned that most of these students are unsuccessful because their learning style is usually ignored in the classroom, not because they lack innate learning ability (Hanson & Dewing, 1990). One reason for this may be that teachers often teach in the way they were taught or in ways that best suit their own learning needs. These ways may not be how their students learn best. Knowing how students are smart and how they learn best are the keys to the doors of possibilities. Students who are not taught in ways that use their unique intelligences and respect their predominant styles of learning are less likely to be successful.

Some may say that this is a simple explanation for lack of school success and that there are many other possible causes. This is true. We all understand that many children do not arrive at school fed, rested, and supported by parents. These and many other circumstances certainly do result in a lack of school success, and much of this is beyond our control. Thankfully, using multiple-intelligences theory and adapting teaching style to meet the needs of learners is not. We have the opportunity to impact kids in a positive way, and we ought to take it. At the very least, schools ought to make every effort to ensure students' success by teaching them in ways that they learn best. Students may overcome the negative circumstances they find themselves in if they can achieve success in school. As the resiliency research shows, schools and teachers are very powerful influences in a child's life, often making the difference between success and failure.

INTRODUCTION TO
MULTIPLE-INTELLIGENCES THEORY

When Gardner (1983) identified the seven intelligences, it was an eye-opener to the field of education. For so long, it was thought that intelligence could be measured by the standard IQ tests with which we are all too familiar. These tests measure intelligence by testing verbal and mathematical skills and aptitude. Gardner is saying that those tests are missing the bigger picture. He asserts that there are at least six other ways to be intelligent: musically, bodily-kinesthetically, spatially, interpersonally, intrapersonally, and naturalistically. Educators ought to take a look at these other ways for the kids' sake, as well as their own, since student success is also teacher success.

Many educators can sadly recall the discouraged students who were not able to do well on traditional academic tasks but who they believed were intelligent and motivated to learn. Try as they might, these students often left school feeling inadequate, convinced that they were not very smart. They seemed to be missing the boat while other students grasped concepts much more easily. Their self-concepts, largely formed by their experiences in school, suffered because the bulk of their experiences taught them that there are only two ways to be smart that matter to the powerful adults and the powerful system of which they were a part. They were not measuring up and they knew it.

Gardner is offering us clues to help us make things better for every student and for teachers, too. Kids can be smart in many ways. The educational system may recognize that fact, but the knowledge is not always put into action. In most cases, teachers are trained to teach without truly perfecting ways to use the eight intelligences to help students learn. Assessments that they use, both standardized and teacher created, mostly rely on linguistic and verbal or mathematical intelligence. Invariably, students who read and write well succeed in most academic areas because being able to comprehend the written word is a skill that transfers to all subject areas. Those who do not read and write well, unless they are labeled and receive resource assistance, may receive low grades as a result. Students who are good at math are lucky because that skill is still highly valued in this society. However, having math skills but lacking the verbal-linguistic skills can still spell trouble for many. It is important not to give up on students who are having trouble reading and writing. Many times, students can learn to read and write well if they are taught to do so by using a variety of strategies, such as entering through the doorway of music, art, or physical action. The wisest teachers are the ones who keep trying alternative methods until one eventually works. My son's fifth-grade teacher did this. She never assumed that an unsuccessful student was not trying hard enough. She herself kept trying until the student was successful.

If home is not supportive and school is a place to experience failure, what is left? Too often kids race from school on their last day and never look back. They are finally free to be themselves and to find success in ways that suit them. Too often, a birth date rather than a graduation ceremony marks their last day. Schools need to address the learning needs of kids who are not mainstream learners before they make such poor choices. We've had Gardner's (1983) clues for some time now, but things are slow to change.

Gardner's theory seems daunting to teachers. How in the world can they assess each person's strongest intelligence and then adapt lessons and devise ways to teach in that way? If students have strong bodily-kinesthetic intelligence, does that mean they can only learn while getting up and moving around, touching objects, or role-playing? If a person is musically smart, does the teacher have to sing the material or put it to music for that student to be successful? These questions may seem silly, but, in fact, many teachers have not tried to incorporate multiple intelligences into their classrooms because these misperceptions persist. Teachers may find this advice from Gardner helpful:

You can say that a child is a visual learner, but that is not a multiple intelligences way of talking about things. What I would say is: "Here is a child who very easily represents things spatially, and we can draw upon that strength if need be when we want to teach the child something new." (cited in Checkley, 1997, p. 13)

When you use students' strengths to help them learn something new, they start out successful. What an idea! Don't we all learn better when we are comfortable and feeling capable?

Gardner (1983) does not suggest that we dispose of reading, writing, and arithmetic in order to concentrate on the content inherent in the other intelligences. He is suggesting that when teaching new content, teachers ought to provide students with opportunities to learn in the way they learn best whenever possible. It is not possible to use all eight intelligences when teaching every piece of content, but it is possible to incorporate more than is the norm currently.

THE EIGHT INTELLIGENCES

Gardner defined seven different ways of being smart. Later, he added the eighth (Checkley, 1997) and leaves open the possibility that there may be more to come. Gardner suggests that intelligence has to do with the ability to solve problems and to produce something that is valued in a particular culture. Gardner provides confirmation for what so many good educators have known for many years: IQ tests are not true pictures of intelligence and schools are not serving their students well when they ignore the many ways that they are or can become intelligent. I am sure that many teachers and counselors are very relieved to have this highly respected Harvard researcher confirm what they have always suspected. While it is too late for many students who left school feeling inadequate and discouraged, now is the perfect time to start to use this important theory more deliberately.

I have summarized the eight intelligences (cited in Checkley, 1997, p. 12):

■ **Verbal and linguistic intelligence** is the capacity to use language, your own and others', to express your thoughts and to understand others' thoughts. A writer, orator, speaker, lawyer, or a person for whom language is an important stock in trade highlights linguistic intelligence.

■ **Logical-mathematical intelligence** is the ability to represent the underlying principles of a causal system, the way a scientist or logician does, or the ability to manipulate numbers, quantities, and operations, as a mathematician does.

■ **Spatial intelligence** is the ability to represent the spatial world internally in your mind the way a sailor or pilot does. Spatial intelligence can be used in the arts or in the sciences. If you are oriented toward the arts, you are likely to become a painter or sculptor. Certain sciences like anatomy or topology emphasize spatial intelligence.

■ **Bodily and kinesthetic intelligence** is the capacity to use your whole body or parts of your body to solve a problem, make something, or put on some kind of production. The most evident examples of people who possess this intelligence are athletes, dancers, actors, or even surgeons.

■ **Musical intelligence** is the capacity to think in music, to be able to hear patterns, recognize them, remember them, and manipulate them. Some people with high degrees of musical intelligence do not play instruments but may use music in purposeful ways. They may even be music critics.

■ **Interpersonal intelligence** is understanding other people. We all need it, but it is at a premium if you are a teacher, clinician, salesperson, or politician.

■ **Intrapersonal intelligence** is understanding yourself, knowing who you are, what you can do, how you react to things, which things to avoid, and which things to gravitate toward.

■ **Naturalist intelligence** refers to the human ability to discriminate among living things (plants and animals), as well as having sensitivity to other features of the natural world (e.g., clouds, rocks). This intelligence was clearly of value when we were hunters and gatherers, and it remains central to roles such as botanist and chef.

HOW AN INTELLIGENCE DEVELOPS

In order to assist the reader in understanding the essential and most practical elements of multiple intelligences theory, I will rely heavily on the work of Armstrong (1994). And I have summarized four of his key points about multiple intelligences theory:

■ **Each person possesses all eight intelligences.** A person does not possess only one intelligence. All people, except those who have suffered severe brain trauma like those in Gardner's research, have capacities in each intelligence, and those intelligences function together in ways unique to each person. Some have higher levels of intelligence in certain areas than others. Some have high levels in all areas. Most of us are highly developed in some intelligences, moderately developed in some, and underdeveloped in the rest.

■ **Most people can develop each intelligence to an adequate level of competency.** If given the appropriate encouragement, enrichment, and instruction, almost all of us can develop all eight intelligences. Many students possess abilities they are unaware of because they have not had opportunities, resources, and support to develop them. Gardner points to the Suzuki method of teaching music as an example of many resources converging to assist the learner, including parent, teacher, exposure to music at an early age, and practice. Multiple intelligences theory considers nurture as well as nature in determining if an intelligence develops.

■ **Intelligences usually work together in complex ways.**
Intelligences are always interacting with one another. For
example, cooking a meal requires linguistic, mathematical,
and interpersonal intelligence. Playing soccer requires bodily-
kinesthetic, spatial, and interpersonal intelligence. The intelligences have been taken out of context only for us to examine
them for their essential features and to learn how to use them
effectively. We must be sure to put them back into context
when we are finished with their study.

■ **There are many ways to be intelligent within each
category.** Some people may not be able to read well but can
tell a great story. Others may not wish to dance but can choreo-
graph a wonderful musical. Multiple intelligences theory
emphasizes that people show their gifts among and within
intelligences.

Armstrong goes on to help us understand what determines
whether a person develops an intelligence. He says that the
development of an intelligence depends on these three things:
biological endowment, personal life history, and cultural and
historical background. He also explains that a person may
have an experience that sparks an intelligence and starts its
development toward maturity. For example, a child may hear
a musical concert and become fascinated with the violin, eventually becoming proficient at it. An athlete may discover the
natural high associated with participating in, and winning,
a race and get hooked on it. These experiences are called *crys-
tallizing* experiences and assist people in finding their niche
in life.

Armstrong also relates that the opposite experience is
called a *paralyzing experience:* An intelligence shuts down
because a person experienced humiliation or failure. These
experiences may be associated with shame or guilt and result
in an intelligence not being developed at all. This may happen, for example, when a child tries to sing and people laugh,
or when an artistic creation is ridiculed. For me, it happened
when I was not successful in a math course and I inferred

from that experience that I was not good at math. I, therefore, learned to avoid it at all costs.

Many Factors Influence Whether an Intelligence Develops

A friend of mine is an audiologist. Until she was well into her 30s, she had no idea that she possessed considerable artistic talent. After taking a drawing course, this aspect of her spatial intelligence soared. She progressed so rapidly that she now supports herself not through audiology but through her artwork. She is a perfect example of the fact that people possess all eight intelligences to some degree. Whether or not they develop depends on many factors. Armstrong (1994) describes these factors as follows:

■ **Access to resources or mentors**. If one were unable to have musical instruments or lessons, one's musical intelligence might not develop.

■ **Historical-cultural factors**. If one lived in a culture which does not allow women to drive, for example, women could not develop that spatial intelligence. Likewise, our young people today have a more highly developed spatial intelligence than their parents due to the long hours spent playing video games which require eye-hand coordination and incredible speed.

■ **Geographical factors**. If people grow up on a lake, they will most likely develop the bodily-kinesthetic intelligence necessary to enjoy that natural resource. Farmers who perform physical labor daily may be more bodily smart than city dwellers.

■ **Familial factors**. Many families encourage or discourage certain interests, depending on their personal experiences. Many parents relate that they do not wish their children to follow in their footsteps, only to have them do just that. (The opposite is also true.) Children may be exposed to a particular career by watching their parents and grow to have a desire to expand their own abilities in that area. Or they may be determined to avoid a career because of their observations.

■ **Situational factors**. Many people just do not have the opportunities provided that would spark an intelligence. Some people, due to physical or mental handicap, may never know if they could have developed an intelligence to any degree. People who have accidents that leave them physically disabled might never know that they possess bodily intelligence in the traditional definition. However, a physically disabled person often must compensate and draw on great physical strength.

We can see from this overview that intelligences develop, or not, for a variety of reasons, some of which have nothing to do with the school environment. Even so, schools are powerful institutions. School is where youths learn, interact, and develop plans for their futures. Schools make assessments about students that set them on a course for life. Many students go through their entire school experiences not knowing how they are smart, unless they are smart in verbal-linguistic and mathematical ways. If they are fortunate enough to have a good art or music teacher, students may have an opportunity to develop those intelligences. If they have opportunities to use their bodies in gym or in sports, they might discover that they are intelligent in that way. Too often, though, students discount the many ways they are smart unless schools place a positive value on them. In addition, teachers miss out on many great teaching opportunities by not discovering their students' unique intelligences.

PUTTING MULTIPLE INTELLIGENCES TO USE

In order to use multiple intelligences, teachers need to know their students. It is not necessary to do time-consuming assessments, but it is necessary to ask questions and observe. Students are eager to tell about themselves. All we have to do is ask. Armstrong (1994) offers some ideas for finding out about students' intelligences. He provides checklists which teachers may use to discover their students' strongest intelligences (see Resource A). He also suggests that teachers may observe how a student misbehaves to find out more about his or her intelligence! (As we will see later in this chapter, we might also find out about students' learning styles in this way as well.) A doodler may excel in spatial intelligence, a talker may excel in interpersonal intelligence, or a jiggler may possess strong bodily-kinesthetic intelligence. Making sure that lessons include opportunities for these spatially, interpersonally, and kinesthetically intelligent students to engage in the learning of new content through mind-mapping, cooperative learning, and movement, for example, will undoubtedly result in fewer disruptions overall. In the quest for knowing your students, finding out how students spend their free time, reviewing school records, and talking with parents and other teachers are strategies that may prove very useful (Armstrong, 1994).

"Know your audience" is an adage to which every successful speaker adheres. Teachers who spend time getting to know their audiences can plan more effectively and avoid many disruptions due to students' lack of engagement. The lesson planning involved in using multiple intelligences does not have to be overwhelming. Moving away from lecture and written responses can actually be fun. Just as with the resiliency attitude, once teachers get a multiple-intelligences attitude, they automatically look for ways to incorporate many different intelligences and flexibly allow students choices to demonstrate what they have learned in multiple-intelligences ways. Doing this ensures that all students get a chance to learn in the best way for them. It also helps students practice their less dominant intelligences.

Sample Task

I use the following very simple task and accompanying table as examples to help graduate students in my class get the resiliency attitude. I believe that whenever we begin to use a new concept, we ought to start simply until we get comfortable. Taking a concept and thinking about different ways of presenting and working with the information is a good way to start. Although counselors do not always teach, they can adapt this technique to activities they do with students:

You are about to teach a unit on the Underground Railroad. Outcomes could include

- An understanding of the causes for the construction of the railroad
- An appreciation for the human toll exacted on the slaves and those who helped them
- An understanding of the economic consequences of the railroad on the South

As you plan activities and assignments to accomplish your goals, how could you use as many of the intelligences as possible?

In Table 3.1 are some activities that correspond to the eight intelligences. Of course, when you apply this approach with something you might teach, activities will vary depending on grade level and subject matter. Once you get started thinking like this, the possibilities are endless.

Choices, Challenges, and Comfort

We have discussed how valuable multiple-intelligences theory is in determining how a struggling student learns best. In order to begin using multiple intelligences theory in the classroom, it is not necessary to individualize instruction for each student at all times. It is necessary, however, to provide students with choices, challenges, and comfort:

- **Choices** provide opportunities for students to make decisions. Making decisions leads to development of an internal-locus control and empowerment. Students who feel they have some control over what happens to them will be more engaged in the learning process.

Table 3.1   Teaching About the Underground Railroad Using the
Eight Intelligences

Intelligences	Sample Tasks Based on Intelligence
Verbal-Linguistic	Students research and write an essay, give a speech, or write a letter about the reasons that the Underground Railroad was created.
Logical-Mathematical	Students accurately determine how many slaves actually used the railroad, how many days and nights were spent during a typical trip, the miles traveled, and so forth. Students may also estimate the impact on the economy due to loss of slave labor.
Bodily-Kinesthetic	Students act out a skit. Students pack a typical bag that slaves carried on their backs and carry it during a role-play which portrays a typical day for a slave on the railroad. Students hide in cramped spots to show how slaves had to hide to avoid capture.
Musical	Students research songs of the period which slaves could have sung as they walked and then play and sing them for class.
Interpersonal	Students work together to speculate on the types of problems that families had during the trip and role play or write about them and even about possible solutions. Students find out what those who hid slaves sacrificed and how they did this.
Intrapersonal	Students reflect on their own views of slavery and if they feel they would have used the railroad to escape. Was it worth the risk? What would they have done?
Spatial	Students draw, sculpt, or otherwise visually represent a day in the life of people on the Underground Railroad.
Naturalist	Students research the ways that the climate, terrain, and natural resources either helped or hindered the slaves as they made their way along the railroad.

■ **Challenges** are key because when a student is challenged, the unspoken message from the teacher is, "I believe you can do this." It is then imperative that the student has the support and resources necessary to be successful.

■ **Comfort** is critically important because whenever any of us is asked to do an unfamiliar task, we leave our comfort zone and our anxiety rises. In order to enhance the chances for successfully teaching new material, a teacher might consider offering opportunities for each child to work in the way that is most comfortable (Silver, Strong, & Perini, 2000).

Using Gardner's example of spatially intelligent children, a teacher, when teaching something new, would use many visuals and allow those children to represent their understanding visually (Checkley, 1997). Depending on their strongest intelligence, allowing other children the options of working in pairs, putting ideas to music, or moving themselves or objects manually might create more comfort for them. On the other hand, if a teacher has created enough trust and safety, asking every student to write a song about a topic may be a good way to practice and nurture musical intelligence, especially if music is not an area of comfort for everyone. Results may be surprising.

Elementary schools may seem to be more conducive to using the multiple intelligences than either middle or high schools because elementary teachers tend to be very creative, have students for extended periods of time, and have smaller bodies to move around a classroom. This may be true, but it is very important that people understand that older students need to have their individuality acknowledged and respected as much as younger students do. As emerging young adults, older students are always seeking ways to be unique, and the wise teacher will capitalize on this need by providing many ways for students to reveal themselves and their ideas.

Providing a wide array of possible tasks and asking students to choose their own is a way of engaging students and allowing them to use their strongest intelligence to learn new material. When assessing, teachers might also consider providing many options for students to demonstrate their understanding of the material. Even though the standardized tests, such as the SAT and state exams, remain with us to evaluate end results, students ought to be able to demonstrate their knowledge during the process in a variety of ways. Writing and singing a song, drawing or sculpting something, verbally giving a report, or acting out a skit could be ways that students could demonstrate knowledge. At the very least, learning would be more enjoyable for students, and they would emerge from school with a better understanding of who they are and what they can do. Gardner says, "School matters, but only insofar as it yields something that can be used once students leave school" (cited in Checkley, 1997, p. 12).

How Learning Styles and Multiple Intelligences Interrelate

In order to fully use Gardner's theory in the school setting, it is important to factor in the theory of learning styles as well. As Silver, Strong, and Perini (2000) point out, multiple intelligences theory focuses on the content of learning and its relation to the disciplines. It does not account for the individualized process of learning. Content is the what of learning and process is the how. We need to consider both. For example, some people may possess musical intelligence but choose not to be performers because their style dictates that they are more suited to composing. One person who is bodily-kinesthetically smart may demonstrate that intelligence by being an athlete, while another may be a massage therapist. I often think of two musically talented people, Mick Jagger and Leonard Bernstein. Maybe it is *style* that accounts for the very different manner in which they manifested their musical intelligences!

There are many tools available to determine one's dominant style of learning and interacting with the world. Silver, Strong, and Perini (2000) believe that teachers and counselors must first understand themselves before they can assist their students. Once they do, they see that there is a complicated interplay between how one learns and what one learns. In order for teachers or counselors to understand students more fully, it is necessary to address both questions: In what ways are students intelligent and how do they learn best?

In the graduate class I teach, I begin each semester by using the True Colors exercise (True Colors Communications Group, 1996) for determining the style of my students (see Resource B). Style relates to learning style as well as preferred style of interacting in all situations. The theory is that everyone possesses characteristics represented by all four colors to some degree, but usually the two strongest colors are the dominant styles exhibited by a person. The choices are blue, gold, green, or orange. The characteristics represented by these colors correspond reasonably well to the styles put forth by Jung and Myers-Briggs (Silver, Strong, & Perini, 2000). Students find the True Colors exercise fun and eye opening, as I do. I feel much more tuned in to the students in my class, and I can then try my best to make sure that I attend to their learning needs. Most of the time, my graduate students are eager to try the test with their own students. They always report that nothing gets their students' attention like finding out about themselves. (See Resource B for the True Colors color assessment tool and Resource C for more information regarding True Colors.)

There are many approaches to styles of learning. All of them overlap to some degree, although not perfectly. When working with youth, the simpler the better. Table 3.2 is a guide to True Colors style.

Once teachers or other educators understand that they have a dominant style, it is much easier to remember that their students do, as well. All students have different preferences for interaction, learning, evaluation, and rewards. For example, mastery style students, or those with gold as their brightest color, perform best in structured, well-defined classrooms with clearly defined expectations which are consistently measured. Interpersonal students, or those with blue as their brightest color, do best in an open, interactive atmosphere with

Table 3.2   Guide to True Colors and Character

True Colors	Key to the Style	Description of the Style
Green	Understanding (Intuitive-Thinking)	Theoretical, knowledge-oriented, intellectual. Analytical, persistent, precise, investigative, logical, rational, ingenious, inventive, needs independence and private time, sets high standards, thorough.
Orange	Self-expressive (Intuitive-Feeling)	Curious, insightful, and imaginative. Self-confident, accepts challenges, takes charge, independent, risk taker, needs variety, learns by doing, seeks high visibility, quick witted, humorous.
Blue	Interpersonal (Sensing-Feeling)	Sociable, friendly, interpersonally oriented. Team player, mediator, sincere, empathic, expressive, leads with feelings, concern for others, appreciates harmony.
Gold	Mastery (Sensing-Thinking)	Realistic, practical, matter of fact Well-organized, prepared, punctual, respects authority and rules, team player, responsible, traditional, trustworthy, prefers structure.

SOURCE: True Colors, Inc., 1996; Silver, Strong, & Perini, 2000.

a teacher who really cares about each student and shows it in a personal way. They thrive on personal feedback and a nurturing, people-oriented environment. Understanding students, or those with green as their brightest color, need to grasp the driving force or theory behind a subject. They prefer to work independently and are energized by new concepts and ideas. They respond positively to recognition and appreciation of their academic performance. Lastly, self-expressive students, or those with orange as their brightest color, generally perform well in competition, especially when there is action involved in the activity. They enjoy fun and excitement and excel in games and hands-on activities. They prefer non-structured, spontaneous presentations and receive gratification from using what they have learned immediately. They seek to apply skills to the world in which they live. With this elemental understanding of the possible styles within a classroom, the question is, "How can educators teach in the most colorful ways?"

Let's go back to the Underground Railroad example. Of the tasks that were offered in Table 3.1, which might appeal to a particular student's style?

■ Mastery learners (gold) enjoy really understanding a topic thoroughly and need to see the practical use for the information. They like structure, predictability, control, and active involvement. They might enjoy the research and essay.

■ Understanding-style learners (green) prefer an intellectual challenge and also prefer to work alone. They are curious, love theory and speculating about future consequences. They might enjoy researching the economic consequences of the loss of slave labor.

■ Interpersonal style learners (blue) prefer to learn about things that directly affect people's lives. They work well when emotionally involved in the task. They might enjoy speculating on the human toll taken by the railroad and slavery on the family.

■ Self-expressive learners (orange) prefer to use their imagination and do the unusual. They do not like rote assignments or routine. They like to find their own solutions. They might enjoy creating a skit or role-play.

As we review the multiple intelligences and learning styles and apply them to the tasks, we could speculate about which students would select particular assignments for some time. However, the important thing is not that we are correct in our speculations. And it is not that the teacher plans an activity for each student, which would certainly be overwhelming. Rather, the important thing is that as we plan to achieve our outcomes, we provide many choices that appeal to different intelligences and learning styles. Students will choose those tasks that hold their interest and feel comfortable. What better way to learn something new? After tasks have been completed, asking students to share their work with the entire class would high-light individuality and reinforce everyone's learning. As Silver, Strong, and Perini (2000) point out, planning ought to take both style and intelligence into consideration.

It's Up To Us

Once again, it falls on the adults in the situation to rise to the occasion. We are, after all, in the powerful position of creating environments. We are the caretakers, if you will, of the content and the process. As resiliency research shows, teachers can and do make a huge difference in kids' lives. Students report that the teachers they loved and respected the most took the time to know them and understand them. Multiple intelligences theory and learning-style theory are two of the tools we have to do this. It is just a matter of using them. Before reading this chapter, the task may have seemed too complicated to start, but I hope that now it does not seem so difficult.

Taking the time at the beginning of the semester to find out who is in the classroom audience is time well spent. It is not enough to plan lessons and activities that tap into various intelligences. To really make a difference, both intelligence and style must be considered. If we want to engage students in their learning, we must treat them as individuals.

> More than what or how they teach, the students valued their teachers for treating them as individuals. As 12th grader Martina Castro puts it, "Education has nothing to do with numbers. Teachers need to connect with us as human beings." (Tell, 2000, p. 12)

Ask the students about themselves and listen to their responses. If you need more structured means, there are many devices available to gather information. The rest is up to us.

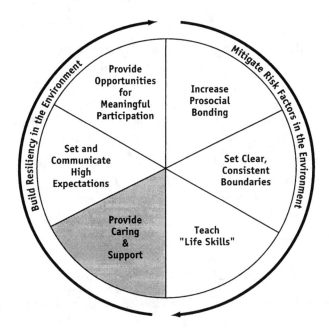

WORKING THE WHEEL

If our goal as educators is to grow healthy, competent people, then there is nothing more important for a student than to feel acknowledged, accepted, and respected. Students who feel this way develop positive self-concept and internal locus of control because they are empowered and self-reliant. On the other hand, students who go unseen often become discouraged, alienated, unmotivated, and disenfranchised. We lose them in a variety of ways, sometimes permanently. If we are embracing a resiliency attitude, then using the multiple-intelligences and learning-style concepts in this chapter make perfect sense. The wheel can help us develop our strategies.

Provide Caring and Support

Students need to trust that their teachers will know them as individuals and that they will take their individual talents and styles into account when working with them. For those students, school is a safe place that has their best interests at heart.

Try This Out With All Ages

■ At the beginning of school or a new semester, give your students a survey or some other instrument to determine their strongest intelligences and preferred learning styles (see Resource B for one option). Facilitate a discussion so that all students get to talk about themselves. To reinforce their understanding of the different intelligences and styles, put visual reminders around the room. That way you and your students can refer to them during the year. This may prove very useful when resolving the conflicts and misunderstandings that inevitably arise. Be sure to include your own style and intelligences, too.

Set and Communicate High Expectations

Teachers who truly believe that each student is unique and who work to draw out the best in each student communicate those high expectations. Students tend to meet our level of expectation.

Try This Out With All Ages

■ This may sound like a time-consuming idea, but it may pay dividends in the end. Have a personal meeting with each student to set a goal or, maybe, a special project. You may want to wait until after the determination of styles so that students may plan projects that will use their strongest intelligences or possibly expand ones that are not so strong. Letting parents know of the students' plans is a great idea so that they might support them. The best part of this is that it sets up a perfect opportunity for a student-run parent conference later in the year.

Provide Opportunities for Meaningful Participation

Students who are given choices within a curriculum which is pertinent and holds meaning for them willingly participate in learning activities, especially when they can make a contribution. Students are eager to assist and eager to make a difference. They just need opportunities to do so.

Try This Out With All Ages

■ Try finding projects or jobs for students that will complement or enhance their styles, such as recruiting the orange, outgoing, interpersonally oriented kids to be visitor greeters at the school's door for a period of time each day. Or try asking the blue, musically inclined students to select mood music for the class during quiet time or reading times. Or try asking the bodily-kinesthetic students to do anything that will get them up and out of their seats legitimately. It is very common for some students to have a balance of colors. For example, some are almost equally blue and orange in their scores. These students are even easier to plan for because you have two opportunities to meet their needs and keep them engaged. Knowing that they possess two equally strong learning or style preferences is an asset to students as they form their self concepts and begin to scan the world for a future place in it.

Increase Prosocial Bonding

Students who believe that school is a caring, meaningful place form positive bonds that assist them in making positive choices regarding friends and school. In addition, techniques such as cooperative learning enhance group cohesion and help kids build resilience.

Try This Out With All Ages

■ Educators could play icebreaker games that not only teach about each other's styles and strongest intelligences but also help students connect. Activities like Find a Person Who . . . are great because kids get to know each other and find common interests and experiences.

Teach Life Skills

Gardner feels that school matters only if it yields something important and useful in the real world. The act of learning about one's multiple intelligences and learning styles is a life skill in and of itself. Insight into one's self and one's behavior is a life skill which employers are eager for (Checkley, 1997).

Try This Out With All Ages

■ In order to learn about your students' multiple intelligences, ask them to play the Find a Person Who . . . game. On a bingo-like card, have a number of different things that people have a preference for, such as: I like to hike and find fossils; I enjoy singing or playing an instrument; I enjoy playing sports; I'd rather read than play video games. Have students talk to each other and write classmates' names in the appropriate squares until the card is filled in. Then share with the entire class. Introduce the eight intelligences and have students talk about how they are smart.

■ In order to introduce your students to the idea of multiple intelligences, ask them to think of famous people and tell how they were smart. For example, President John F. Kennedy, Albert Einstein, Michael Jordan, Robert Frost, Janet Reno, Julie Andrews, Hillary Clinton, Britney Spears. Use this as a starting point to talk about how people can be smart. Ask them to think about how they are smart. Then tell about the eight intelligences.

■ A very simple way to introduce multiple intelligences to reluctant adolescents who do not have insight into how they are smart is to create a chart with the names of famous people (be sensitive to a balance of genders and ethnic groups) who exhibit a particular intelligence. Leave space for the students to add their names. Ask students to place their names in the box that has the names of people who interest them, whom they admire and wish to be like. Then ask them about their choices and let them talk.

■ Keep the names of the multiple intelligences visible, with a picture of a person who exhibits each intelligence so that students make the connections.

■ Use a tool with students to determine their preferred style of interaction. Spend time with them processing this information and determining what it means.

■ Have students bake chocolate chip cookies for homework, and the next day, identify how many intelligences are used in this one activity. And then enjoy the cookies!

■ Remember, if a student is having trouble learning decimals the way you are teaching them, try a different way. Put the rules to a rap song, or line up students and have them hold numbers and a decimal point. Ask students to take turns placing the decimal in the right spot.

■ Remember to always use the child's strongest intelligence and preferred style of learning when teaching something new.

Summary

Just as with character education, when the theories of multiple intelligences and learning styles are boiled down to their essences, they are not so overwhelming. Also, the connection to building resiliency in students becomes clear once we understand how integral these movements are to preparation for life. Finding out how individual students are smart and then using that information to help them learn is an approach that builds resilience. Students who are successful in school possess the potential for a bright future. Those who experience school failure are at great risk. We cannot let students fail without trying everything possible to assist them.

Once teachers get comfortable thinking about styles and different ways of being smart, planning to accommodate students becomes second nature. Teachers who truly believe that all kids can learn keep searching for ways to reach them until they are successful. Before educators get started using these wonderful concepts, it is important that they understand their own strengths. Only then can they assist their students in understanding theirs. So find out about yourselves and then find out who is in your audience. Remember, just the act of asking students about themselves builds resilience. You are assisting them in understanding themselves for life. Students enjoy the process and become partners in learning rather than consumers of subject content.

4

Emotional Intelligence and Building Resilience

What factors are at play, for example, when people of high IQ flounder and those of modest IQ do surprisingly well? I would argue that the difference quite often lies in the abilities called here emotional intelligence which include self-control, zeal and persistence, and the ability to motivate oneself. And these skills, as we shall see, can be taught to children, giving them a better chance to use whatever intellectual potential the genetic lottery may have given them.

—Daniel Goleman (1995, p. xii)

Both emotional literacy and emotional intelligence are important because having the potential for positive emotional growth without the opportunity to develop it at a skill level is of little practical value. Intelligence is potential while literacy is skill. A person may possess the potential for developing quality social interaction, but if that ability is not developed and nourished through practice, it will not be available to the person when it is needed. The ability to recognize and manage one's emotions is a skill that is used and, hopefully, honed throughout one's lifetime. If I reflect on the people with whom I most enjoy spending time and working, they are those who are interpersonally astute, intrapersonally aware, caring, humorous, and trustworthy. As we have read in previous chapters, these interpersonal attributes are ones that resilient people possess.

EMOTION IS THE KEY

Many years ago, when I first began working in the field of drug and alcohol abuse prevention, I realized that if we want to prevent kids from abusing substances, we have to help them cope with their emotions in positive ways. The root cause of almost every adolescent's substance abuse is a problem with family dysfunction, social failure, school failure, and personal failure. Every recommended prevention strategy in some way addresses the emotional issues that place kids at risk of using substances. These are prevention strategies such as life skills classes or groups, conflict resolution and peer mediation, peer pressure refusal skills, peer leadership, positive alternatives, and crisis counseling. All of these strategies have the same goal: to assist students in developing personal and interpersonal skills so that they can navigate the world safely without the need to rely on alcohol or other drugs for support.

Prevention work centers on emotions: how to recognize them and how to handle them in real life situations. If we accept that the role of education is to prepare young people for life and not just for exams, then it would be safe to say that education ought to consider the emotional side of learning. Until Goleman (1995) introduced the idea of a link between emotions and learning, few people considered addressing socioemotional issues as they related to the ability to learn.

Goleman finally confirmed the importance of attending to a student's emotional state. In addition to helping us understand how the brain works, he also suggests that in life, people's ability to successfully interact socially is possibly more important than her or his ability to solve quadratic equations. Acknowledging and assisting students with social and emotional needs actually enhances their chances for academic success. The link between the ability to learn and the ability to manage emotions is becoming clearer as more is learned about brain-based learning. "But in the classroom, a student can perceive even a mild stressor to be threatening, initiating the stress response and lessening the student's ability to perform" (Wolfe, 2001, p. 110).

Schools often rely on counselors to "educate the affect," as Goleman (1995) says, while teachers focus on teaching subject matter. This is a mistake in two ways. First, there are not enough counselors to do this huge job, and second, teachers who view their jobs as solely teaching subject matter are potentially making their jobs more difficult. As we will see later in this chapter, students who are struggling with emotional issues cannot learn to their potential. If educators focus simultaneously on the affect and the subject content, they prepare students for school success and for life success as well. Emotional aptitude is a meta-ability and determines how well we can use other skills, including raw intellect (Goleman, 1995). "Emotion is a double-edged sword, with the ability to enhance learning or impede it" (Wolfe, 2001, p. 111). This chapter will lay a foundation for understanding the physiology of emotions, key assumptions about emotions, and how we can use this knowledge to help us build resiliency in students.

EMOTIONAL INTELLIGENCE THEORY

Goleman (1995) asserts that having or lacking emotional intelligence can mean success or failure for a person, regardless of IQ. In fact, he stated that emotional intelligence is "at times more powerful" than IQ (p. 34). As you can imagine, this assertion created quite a stir. Some people were excited by the prospect that it was all right to talk about and try to impact socioemotional behavior. In fact, many schools adopted programs to foster emotional intelligence and were very willing to accept Goleman's premise before long-term research could determine if he was correct.

Others, like Cobb and Mayer (2000), undertook research projects to scrutinize the idea more closely. Cobb and Mayer discuss what the research says about the existence of emotional intelligence:

> Early findings provide strong evidence that emotional intelligence looks and behaves like other intelligences, such as verbal intelligence, but remains distinct enough to stand alone as a separate mental ability. Like other intelligences, emotional intelligence appears to develop with age. (Cobb & Mayer, 2000, p. 17)

Two Models of Emotional Intelligence

Cobb and Mayer (2000) define two models of emotional intelligence: the ability model and the mixed model. The ability model "defines emotional intelligence as a set of abilities and makes claims about the importance of emotional information and the potential uses of reasoning well with that information" (p. 15). According to these authors, the ability model means that you learn how to identify and deal effectively with emotions—yours and others'. It is like learning how to cook and being able to make a meal out of anything. The mixed model "is more popularly oriented. It mixes emotional intelligence as an ability with social competencies, traits, and behavior, and makes wondrous claims about the success this intelligence leads to" (p. 15). In other words, the mixed model sets out a core set of skills to be learned, as in a curriculum. Often, promoters of curricula claim that simply adhering to the objectives and lessons within the curriculum will ensure that students will acquire the skills of emotional literacy and will, therefore, be more likely to succeed now and in the future. The truth lies somewhere in between. It is necessary for people to learn the skills of emotional literacy. This is often accomplished within a curriculum. Students often need instruction in the specifics of emotional literacy. They do need to acquire a set of diverse tools, if you will, that they can use to interact successfully with others. Having limited tools for emotional literacy is of little value in a complex world. In order to be successful, the key is, as with all good education, that students be able to practice in realistic ways so that they can transfer this learning to the real world. Students require a set of tools, and they must be able to know which tool is appropriate for which task.

The comparison of two types of emotional intelligence models reminds me of Kohn's (1997) comparison of the two types of character education, narrow and broad. The ability model, like the broad model, does not come with prescriptions for actions. This model encourages us to use the information we have about emotional intelligence to create environments and experiences for students so that they may develop their emotional intelligence skills, or their emotional literacy. We ought to be encouraging our students to identify feelings, understand their origins, and deal effectively with them. "The logic behind the ability model [was] that emotions are signals about relationships. For example, sadness signals loss" (Cobb & Mayer, 2000, p. 14). It is important to recognize the inside emotion behind the outward emotion. Students who possess insight into their feelings are more likely to remain in control of them.

Emotional Intelligence Can Be Developed

Emotional intelligence encompasses two of the multiple intelligences, interpersonal and intrapersonal. It is an integral part of character education, and I believe it is the core of resiliency. The ability model emphasizes that emotional intelligence actually does exist, and if it is a standard intelligence (like general IQ), then people who are emotionally intelligent might be engaged in a sophisticated process. "The concept of emotional intelligence legitimizes the discussion of emotions in schools and other organizations because emotions reflect crucial information about relationships" (Cobb & Mayer, 2000, p. 15).

In the previous chapter, we learned that, according to Gardner, all of us possess at least eight different intelligences, to some degree. Some of us are naturally more gifted in certain areas, and some of us have just had more opportunities to develop our intelligences. That means that, even though they may possess innate emotional intelligence, many children are growing up in homes and community environments that do not provide the best context for learning how to handle emotions. Thankfully, educators can assist students in developing their emotional intelligence and their emotional literacy in multitudinous ways. Many of the characteristics of resilient people have to do with social competence: ability to elicit positive response, communication skills, ability to think reflectively, ability to form positive relationships. These are traits that can be acquired with guidance, and educators can and do play a big part in this effort (Benard, 1991).

Salovey and Mayer (1990) first proposed a model of emotional intelligence that divides emotional intelligence into five domains. Goleman (1995) follows their model. Salovey and Mayer's five domains are

- *Knowing one's emotions:* self-awareness, recognizing a feeling as it happens
- *Managing one's emotions:* handling feelings in an appropriate way
- *Motivating oneself:* marshaling emotions in the service of a goal, emotional self-control, delaying gratification
- *Recognizing emotions in others:* empathy
- *Handling relationships:* managing emotions in others

Emotional Intelligence Is Also the Core of Character Education

This approach may remind you of Lickona's (1991) character education model in Chapter 2. Lickona speaks of moral knowing, moral feeling, and moral action, and specifies within each of the three areas the actions and knowledge necessary for building character. In essence, educating for character is the same as educating for emotional literacy. This seems a bit like a proof from geometry class: If educating for character is the same as educating for emotional literacy, and educating for character is also the same as educating for resiliency, then educating for emotional literacy is the same as educating for resiliency. In other words, these megatrends are all related. Lickona has said, "We need to be in control of ourselves—our appetites, our passions—to do right by others. It takes will to keep emotion under the control of reason" (cited in Goleman, 1995, p. 285).

In light of school shootings, e-mail threats, bomb scares, adolescent suicides, teen pregnancy, drug addiction, and gang violence, to name a few examples, it is clear that our young people are in need of assistance when it comes to handling emotions. In fact, when one reflects on the growing problems of road rage and addiction in the adult segment of our society, it is clear that the apples have not fallen far from the trees, as my dad used to say. Again, some people do not develop certain intelligences because instruction through role models and opportunities to practice do not exist. We are a society that appears to be losing ground in the area of emotional intelligence. The development of the two intelligences that make up emotional intelligence, interpersonal and intrapersonal, are critical. Students need to have the opportunity to develop the set of skills that they can use to put their intelligence into action in order to be considered emotionally literate.

Bocchino (1999) defines emotional literacy this way:

> It is, in part, the ability to decode cues, whether they are printed cues on a page of text or the subtle cues of interpersonal communication. Moreover, literacy includes skills for creating meaning and the ability to apply that understanding to our own lives. Also, literacy is the ability to communicate fluently. And, ultimately, being literate must include a constellation of cultural and personal maps that help us to understand not only the world around us but also ourselves. (p. xiii)

THE PHYSIOLOGY OF EMOTIONS

The human brain has evolved over the past 500,000 years. Evolution is a slow process, and our physical brains have not kept pace with the products of our brainpower. In just two centuries, even though our nation has gone from horses to model Ts to Mars, we are still navigating with the brain that helped us to survive in primitive times. It can sabotage us today if we are not careful. We often confront modern dilemmas with an ancient emotional repertoire (Goleman, 1995).

Much has been written recently about brain development and its relationship to learning. More is currently being written about what could possibly lead youngsters to shoot fellow classmates or friends. We are shocked each time this happens and are left wondering if people are born violent or if they become that way. One thing is certain, the emotionally charged mind easily fools people. Upset people do things on impulse that they would never do in a calmer, more rational state of mind. In order to avoid living in a reactive state, we all need the skills, or emotional literacy, to be able to understand and intercept emotions before they become troublesome. Adolescents are at considerable risk because their brains are not yet fully developed. They do not have the same resources or life experiences to draw on as adults do when faced with emotionally charged situations.

In the distant past, we survived because we reacted quickly and accurately in response to threat. To this day, our brain is programmed to protect us from danger, whether perceived or real, emotional or physical. As we move through our lives on a daily basis, our emotional responses are shaped by rational judgment (perceiving and assessing facts), personal history (what has happened to shape us), and our ancestral past (our neurobiology) (Goleman, 1995). For better or worse, these three factors operate simultaneously and often do so without relying too heavily on current facts. For example, people who have experienced a trauma of some kind will very likely react with great emotion and physical responses when experiencing a trigger for the memory, even though their current situation may be safe. Their bodies may react in physical ways, such as increased heartbeat or sweaty palms, because their brains have sent signals that they are in danger. Their bodies cooperate by getting ready to defend themselves. War veterans who have experienced posttraumatic stress disorder understand this seeming irrational response, as do children who have experienced abuse. In a paradoxical way, the brain's response is very rational, because the trigger for the physical response is perceived as real. When this happens, the brain goes into survival mode and the body responds. As we will see, this helpful brain can often create havoc for students.

How the Brain Developed: Our Ancestral Past

In a nutshell, the human brain has evolved over millions of years, starting with the reptilian brain and adding structures and associated abilities, such as the limbic system and neocortex. The reptilian part of the brain basically maintains automatic functions, such as breathing, digestion, and other involuntary systems. In addition, it controls hunger, mating urges, fight or flight response, and territoriality. Some people seem to stake out their pews in church, for example. If another sits in the pew, unaware that it has been claimed, there is often a palpable tension as the former inhabitant dejectedly looks for a new seat. Now think of school cafeterias and the problems that arise when one student takes another's seat. This is when the reptilian brain kicks into gear, and, as we shall see later in this chapter, logic and reasoning are often placed on the back burner.

According to MacLean (1990), after the reptilian brain, the paleomammalian (cortex, limbic) brain developed next, almost on top of the reptilian brain. The limbic system refines two powerful tools: learning and memory (Goleman, 1995). Unlike reptiles, mammals are nurturing to their young, while reptiles eat theirs on occasion. We've all seen dogs, cats, whales, and other mammals nurture and protect their young, and we are drawn to them because we value this in ourselves. Mammals interact and feel connection to each other. They are more curious and discerning and, consequently, make better choices that enhance their chances for survival. They establish social hierarchy and actually exhibit signs of altruism, such as when female dogs nurse the pups of other dogs that have been disabled or killed.

The newest part of the brain is the neocortex, almost triple the size of our nearest primate cousins and unique to human beings. This structure allows us to metacogitate—or think about our thinking. We can solve problems, reflect on past experiences, and predict future situations. We can invent, write, read, speak, and even harness Mother Nature herself. The neocortex separates humans from all other animals. However, the other parts of our more primitive brain remain with us, and we must take them and their functions into account if we want to understand behavior and the part emotions play in it. Lest we get too full of ourselves, we must remember that the reptilian (survival) brain is still with us in a big way.

Separating the brain into three segments according to when they developed may seem to suggest that when one brain was no longer useful, we grew a better one, and the old brain is not playing a part in how we think and behave. Actually, the brains, if you will, interact all the time. The reptilian brain, located in the brain stem, continues to signal our bodies to breathe and digest our food. The limbic system, including both the amygdala and hippocampus, continues to generate emotional responses. In fact, emotional areas are intertwined neurologically into all areas of the neocortex, giving the emotional centers immense powers over the rest of the brain, including the centers for thought. To this day, the limbic structures do most of the brain's learning and remembering (Bocchino, 1999; Goleman, 1995).

The Power of the Amygdala

The limbic brain has a structure called the amygdala, which is located just above the brain stem. Neuroscientist Joseph LeDoux found that the amygdala can perceive things that trigger strong emotions, such as fear or rage, before the rational part of the brain does (Goleman, 1995, p. 18). This small, almond shaped structure holds immense power. If you lack this structure in your brain, you lose your hardwired ability to respond with fear. Even in a life-threatening situation, you would remain unaroused for fight or flight. The amygdala is a sentinel. When it registers fear, the body reacts physiologically. It responds to physical or emotional triggers and drives the rest of the brain during an emergency. Most mothers can remember a time when they pulled their child away from danger, such as when a car was approaching too fast. Afterward, they might not know exactly what or how they knew what to do, but just acted. This is how the brain can help us. The amygdala holds a privileged position in that, when aroused, it responds before the neocortex does, which means before a more thoughtful response can be generated. If the mother stopped to think and consider all the possibilities she had, her child might have died.

The interplay of the reptilian brain, the limbic system, and the neocortex is the heart of emotional intelligence. The limbic structures retain the emotional flavor that goes with facts (Bocchino, 1999; Goleman, 1995). Life would be very boring if all we were concerned with was the facts. We'd all be like robots. We need and want the limbic system to compliment the rational side of our brains. The key is to remain in balance with our emotions, and to do this, it is necessary to be emotionally literate. We need to know how to recognize emotions in ourselves and others, and we need the skills to deal with those emotions effectively.

As you can imagine, the implications of this information for students, teachers, counselors, and administrators are enormous. Any time a student (or anyone) experiences a trigger for a strong emotional response, the rational (thinking) side of the brain takes a back seat. Students are unable to access their working memory at times like these. Therefore children who arrive at school angry or afraid are not ready to learn. Children who become frustrated or sad during school will have their learning interrupted until the emotional upset is resolved. As we all know, life is not always rosy for kids.

Kids arrive with their backpacks full of books and their heads full of their most recent life experiences, good and bad. They experience the effects of divorce, loss, violence, neglect, conflict, bullying, and stress as deeply as adults do. Educators who are sensitive to, and deal with, this reality will enhance their students' chances for success. If we understand how the emotional brain works, both physically and mentally, and how it can interrupt the learning process, we can help students learn to recognize physical and environmental cues to help them manage emotions better.

PUTTING EMOTIONAL INTELLIGENCE THEORY INTO USE

Goleman's (1995) key concepts regarding the brain can help us apply this knowledge to the school setting. They are summarized below.

The emotional mind is quicker than the rational mind. We've all had the experience of being startled when something unexpected pops out at us. Our bodies react physically because the brain sends a signal in a split second that something is amiss. We jump, our hearts race, and adrenaline starts to pump into our muscles so we can fight or flee. This worked great for us when bears lurked behind bushes. It may not be so helpful in a middle school corridor. Students who are interacting in a school setting are doing so on many different social and academic levels. At the middle and high school levels, youngsters are usually as concerned with appearance, popularity, and self-protection as they are with academics. Additionally, far too many students arrive in school still reeling from their home experiences that may include dealing with alcoholic or drug-abusing parents and siblings, parental job loss or economic problems, other family problems, or neglect. These issues may place them in a negative emotional state. A look, gesture, or word could easily be misinterpreted as a threat or rejection. A quiet or shy student's response may be to withdraw and brood for a time, ruining any chance for paying attention to class material. Another student may react more aggressively and strike out verbally or physically, usually starting a long and unpleasant chain of events. As we just read, the emotional brain responds before a more thoughtful response can be generated. If students lack skills for generating more thoughtful responses, problems usually escalate.

When we are emotionally aroused, our actions carry a sense of certainty. Later, we might say, "What was I thinking?" How many times have we scolded a child or reacted to a spouse, so sure we were right, only to reflect later and wish we had waited a day to react? How often are students confronted with gossip, rumors, teasing, bullying, ostracism, and other forms of aggression? How often have best friends sworn never to speak to one another again? How important is it for adolescents to save face? Is it any wonder students get into conflicts on a daily basis? Students who are brought into the office because of an altercation often tell very different stories of the incident, but each one believes he or she is telling the truth. Both are certain that things happened the way they remember. Sound familiar? This is often due to the fact that memories can be tainted because of emotional arousal, and, when aroused, we are certain that we remember correctly. Only after calming down can we think clearly and see another's point of view. This is why angry students cannot be expected to sit down and talk rationally. They need time to walk around and cool off before anyone, including an authority figure like the principal, tries to do an intervention.

Emotions sacrifice accuracy for speed. When we are emotional, we react first and think later. That is probably where the term *second thoughts* comes from. Students enter counselors' offices saying, "He said!" or "She said!" or "I don't like the way they're looking at me!" On closer inspection, teachers and counselors often find that the students making these statements are often not totally sure what they are reacting to at all, other than hurt feelings. When a teacher or counselor mediates two students having a conflict, it is often possible to defuse it by adding some facts. When students have the opportunity to explain their actions or their perceptions to each other, it is often possible for feelings to be soothed and life to go on peacefully.

Recently, a counselor told me that she had been asked to speak to two girls who could not get along in gym. One was being very aggressive toward the other, and things were getting explosive. Once given the opportunity to speak their piece, it turned out that the problem was that the aggressive student was jealous because the other girl had nicer clothes and things than she had. With this out on the table, the girls were able to reach an understanding and actually found that they *wanted* to like each other, but until this talk, they did not feel that it could be possible. Maybe with this new understanding, it will be.

Emotions choose us. We do not choose them. When we find ourselves angry, sad, happy, or anxious we often have to think about why. We feel a certain way and ask, "What is it about this situation that makes me feel this way?" Youngsters do not always have words to describe what they are feeling. They may not even recognize what has triggered the emotion. That is because everyone's brain stores memories of all kinds: smells, sights, songs, spoken words. Long before language is developed, infants are storing memories that imprint on their brains and have an impact on future behavior. Neglect and abuse impact a child's ability to trust and form bonds with others. A child may not be able to articulate the experiences that caused this problem, but the effect on social development is still present and powerful. Students need to know how to recognize triggers or recognize their bodies' responses, and know how to change the way they feel in positive ways. In other words, they need to be in self control.

Emotions are associative. Long before the written word, people told stories. Stories of heroines and heroes, of compassionate actions, of love and romance, of tragedy and loss hook us emotionally, and we pay attention. Stories communicate feeling and emotions, and that is why people remember them. Have you had the experience of being able to remember what speakers said because they used stories to illustrate a point? Or maybe you remember the story, and from that you are able to recall the point it illustrated. The important thing is that when it comes to feelings, we can relate. The more scared or excited or emotionally involved we are when something happens, the better we remember it. That is why all the baby boomers I know can remember where they were on the day President John F. Kennedy was assassinated. That is why most people can remember their first date—good or bad. That is also why excellent and wise teachers make their subject content meaningful to their students' lives so that they will personalize it in some way and remember it better. I once had a history professor in college who presented information as if it were a soap opera. He put the facts into stories, and the people we were learning about came to life. How much easier it is to remember what people did when we can relate to them as human beings. This professor's personalized stories helped us to feel what others must have felt, and so we remember the important event.

Emotions cause us to react to the present as if it were the past. All experiences, good and bad, are imprinted on our brains somewhere. The smell of a turkey cooking might bring up pleasant memories and place us in a positive emotional state. The smell of a pencil and eraser or the sight of a particular classroom might bring up past memories of poor performance on an exam and create anxiety that can interfere with present circumstances. Students may dislike a teacher who reminds them of another who hurt them, and they may not even realize that this is affecting their attitude. Students who have experienced difficulty early in their school careers may associate tests with failure, and have anxiety that will make future success even more difficult. A bad experience with a bully may taint a child's ability to form social bonds with others. On the other hand, positive experiences with teachers and other students create a set of expectations for positive futures.

The emotional mind is state specific. A person will react one way when angry, another way when sad or happy. This seems to be self-explanatory, but things can get confusing. We tend to notice when someone's words and emotional state seem incongruous. For example, when people assure you they are fine with a decision as they struggle to keep back tears. Or some people may swear they are not angry while veins are popping out on the side of their temples. This contradiction is confusing for everyone, especially the people and their poor bodies. Often, when people lack emotional literacy, they may not recognize their feelings, and, as a result, they are held hostage to them. A key component of emotional intelligence is the ability to identify feelings and effectively deal with them. Those who do not learn to be emotionally literate are at risk not only for negative social consequences but also for physical problems. As we have learned, the body reacts to the brain's instructions. Anger, fear, sadness, or disappointment put negative physical stress on many systems in the body. Laughter, on the other hand, releases good brain chemicals (endorphins), which can actually help us learn and heal physically.

The emotional mind is usually in balance with the rational mind. However, when passions surge, the emotional mind gets the upper hand. This may account for some crimes of passion or suicides. People literally are out of their rational minds. As Goleman (1995) relates, there are many murderers who started out as burglars, but when the panic of being caught took over, they killed their victims to avoid that possibility. In a school setting, I am sure that students of all ages would prefer success to failure, calm to upset, and happy to sad, but thoughts, words, and experiences often tip the scales in favor of negative emotions. Only with role models, self-knowledge, and practice will students be able to balance emotions with rationality.

WORKING THE WHEEL

Now that we better understand emotions and the brain's part in them, it is easier to grasp that once again, the school

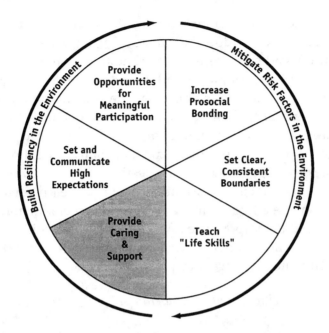

environment can promote or hinder the development of emotional intelligence and the skills for emotional literacy. Through our actions and the environments we create, we can teach students the skills to maintain their emotional balance. Without purchasing a curriculum or devoting precious class time to extra lessons on emotional intelligence, teachers and counselors can weave emotional-skill development into daily interactions with their students. Using the wheel as a guide for creating strategies to do this is very helpful.

Provide Caring and Support

Students who believe that their feelings matter are more likely to think that other peoples' feelings matter, as well. Those who show care and respect for their students usually receive it in return. For example, a teacher who took my graduate class began to implement strategies that showed care and support for her third-grade students as her project. By her own admission, prior to this, she had not considered that children were entering her classroom each day with their emotional baggage in tow. She began to smile at the children more and tried to show them more patience. When a student asked, "Why do I have to do this?" instead of impatiently saying, "Because I said so," she took the time to give the student an explanation for the logic behind the assignments. She tried to assist her students in making what she was teaching personally meaningful to them. Once students understand the why, they are more willing to move forward. She reported that the change in her students was amazing. Simply treating each child respectfully, reacting to questions and behavior with patience, and making information they must learn personally relevant made a huge difference in class climate. In addition, she realized the importance of giving children a voice in decisions and plans to begin next year very differently. Never underestimate the power of a positive attitude.

Try This Out With Secondary Students

■ Regularly, maybe once per week, ask if there is anyone with a classroom issue to discuss. Issues should not be personal but could relate to the amount of homework given, anticipation of tests, noise level, messiness, overall behavior, and so forth. Alot a specific amount of time for discussion and problem solving, and allow the students the opportunity to express their feelings. Facilitate the discussion and explain your rationale for any actions you take to help remedy the situations. There may be some things that are nonnegotiable. However, if students feel that they have a voice in the decisions that affect their lives, they will be more likely to accept rules and standards as their own. Modeling flexibility teaches flexibility. Helping students understand the *why* behind the *what* of what they are required to do prepares them for real-life situations (such as paying taxes).

■ Before each class, ask this: "On a scale of 1 to 10, how is everyone feeling today?" Let all students give their numbers verbally or, maybe, even hold up a paper with the number written on it so that there is a degree of privacy. Be sure to add your own. You will immediately get an idea of how class might go that day. If many people are feeling quite low, spend a few minutes discussing why. If one or two students are low, you might ask them after class if there is anything you could help with. High school students would benefit from the teacher explaining why this exercise is important so that they can gain an awareness of how emotions impact learning. They will take this knowledge along to work or college.

Try This Out With Elementary or Middle School Students

■ Younger children like to place a mark on a thermometer or some other visual to show how they are feeling. They could make and keep a mood thermometer on their desks so that as you circle the room, you could see how they are feeling that day. Noting and commenting as the temperatures go up and down may be a good way to start meaningful conversations. Taking the time to attend to emotional temperatures is a great way to show you care, offer support, and assist students in understanding that it is best to deal up-front with issues or problems, because they will interfere with our lives (and learning) until we do. Five or 10 minutes up-front each morning may allow for more valuable instruction time during the remainder of the class. Remember, emotions can block the rational side of the brain and interfere with learning.

■ Another simple strategy is finding out about personal issues students are experiencing, such as divorce or the death or illness of a parent, grandparent, or pet. Although doing this may seem like common sense, teachers and counselors often are the last to know when students are having personal crises. Sometimes, educators have to put their antennae on and seek out students who seem withdrawn or distracted to ask them why. It may be possible to connect the student to a counselor or offer support both personally and, if appropriate, from the entire class. Students will feel that people care, and they may be more likely to stay focused on schoolwork when they know that there is an outlet for their feelings.

■ Sometimes, something as simple as going outside for a walk while you talk communicates that you are serious about building a relationship. I know a counselor who swung on the swings with a middle school girl who didn't want to talk. Swinging helped her to open up and talk about her feelings. Being willing to meet kids on neutral turf communicates a genuine willingness to connect with them.

Set and Communicate High Expectations

For better or for worse, emotions have a large effect on achievement. As we just read, when the brain is preoccupied with fear, anxiety, or any other powerful emotion, students are less able to access their working memories. "Blanking out" on tests is a frustrating phenomenon because often students can easily recall the facts once the test is over. Educators can assist students in keeping emotions in check so that they are able to do their best work.

Try This Out With Any Grade Level

■ Help students identify where in their bodies they feel their fear or anxiety. Often, it will be in their stomachs or their extremities, but people vary. Once identified, assist your students in breathing techniques that will relax and refocus the brain. Have them breathe in deeply through their noses and exhale through their mouths for three or four repetitions. Have them stand and shake their hands and feet and wiggle around at their seats. Every time a student moves in a physical way, the brain responds. It gets more blood and oxygen, and it changes the mental state it is in. These exercises are good to do even when a test is not about to be taken.

■ Students need to believe that they can do it. All types of athletic teams have rituals that create positive energy. In huddles, team members touch hands and shout a word that puts their minds in a positive state. Educators can do the same thing. Classrooms can spend a few minutes getting into a *game* state of mind where students believe they are prepared and are able to meet a challenge.

■ Any skill that a teacher or counselor can impart that will help students move through a test without becoming rattled or discouraged will benefit student achievement. For example, if a student does not know an answer, instead of getting frightened and allowing negative emotion to creep into the brain, teach students to mark the question and tell themselves that they know the answer and that they will come back to it in a few minutes. Very often, focusing on something else will allow the brain time to retrieve the information it was looking for.

Provide Opportunities for Meaningful Participation

I can think of no better way for students to develop empathy than to experience another's perspective of the world. Young people are developmentally self-centered, which is not to say selfish but, rather, that they perceive the world from their own perspectives. They usually do not understand what they have not experienced. Therefore offering them opportunities that will help them to become more aware of the feelings of others will assist them in developing empathy. Educators might try some simple strategies that can easily be integrated into a language arts or social studies curriculum.

Try This Out With Middle or Secondary Students

■ Ask students to think of people they know personally (or maybe book characters) who are different from them in some way. They might be old, foreign, ill, new to school, a different race, and so forth. Assign a pretend interview in which students ask their real or imagined person a group of questions. Maybe the class will brainstorm questions everyone would like to know about. The interviewer then answers the questions themselves, based on their perceptions. A question might be, "What do you do for fun?" The interviewers then answer the question based on what they think might be true. Class discussion could focus on these answers, and students could talk about the feasibility of the answers. If possible, the students could then conduct actual interviews and write about the similarities and differences between their perceptions and reality.

■ Conduct a day when students get to experience what it feels like to be old, deaf, blind, wheelchair-bound, bullied, ostracized, a different race, and so forth. They could also think about how Civil War soldiers felt during the winter, or how those who fought in Vietnam felt, or how the parents of a soldier felt, and so forth. Simulate situations for a whole day in which students get to feel what others feel. Offer students ways to express their understanding of others' experiences. Role-plays, music, writings, verbal expressions, and so forth.

Try This Out With Elementary Students

■ Create opportunities for your students to help others. They could be the buddies for new students who make sure that new kids adjust well and have a lunch partner. They could help younger students who are struggling with subjects. They could assist younger students in acquiring gym skills. Whatever the task, it is important that there is an opportunity for the student to process the experience with an adult. Through this discussion, students can develop empathy and identify their own feelings during the process.

Increase Prosocial Bonding

Students who feel welcome and appreciated for their uniqueness are more likely to bond to school. As educators, how can we communicate to our students that we like and respect them? It is helpful to reflect on what people are doing when we ourselves feel liked and respected. For me, when someone remembers my name or something about me, I feel good. I feel that person really saw me and thought I was worth remembering. This makes me want to interact with that person again and, even more important, it teaches me to do the same for someone else. Role modeling teaches students ways to make people feel welcome. Sometimes the home is not teaching skills like this, so educators are, once again, picking up the slack.

Try This Out With All Ages

■ Welcome students to your class and make a point to mention something personal to at least 10 different students during the course of the day. Notice new shoes, different hairstyles, a book they have that you also enjoyed, a musical group you notice they enjoy, and so forth. Make it a game with yourself where you try to beat your best day.

■ Know your students' names and use them by the end of the first month of school.

Teach Life Skills

If Goleman (1995) and Bocchino (1999) are correct, then skills of emotional literacy are skills for life. The more we can do to assist students in identifying and managing their emotions, the better. All of the strategies listed in this book so far assist with this endeavor.

Try This Out With Elementary Students

■ In elementary grades, teach students names for how they feel, such as angry, fearful, disappointed, excited, sad, happy, frustrated, and so forth. In addition, let them practice identifying faces that are expressing these emotions. Some researchers have suggested that playground bullies seem to lack empathy. In addition, they needed assistance in learning how to read people's faces. Once they received this instruction during an intervention, they stopped the bullying behavior (Poole, 1997).

■ Spend time assisting students in recognizing, naming, and owning their emotions. Let students role-play an emotion, and let other students guess what it is.

■ When reading stories, ask students, "What is this character feeling?" and "How do you know this?" Many educators are probably reading this right now and thinking, "I already do this," and I am sure you are right. Kids need all the practice they can get. I would simply encourage you to do this more often and more deliberately, especially for children from high-risk environments who might lack role models and adults to talk to about their feelings.

■ Reserve a corner of the classroom for conflict resolution. There are important preliminary actions to take before using this strategy, and there are many good books and resources for step-by-step instruction. Both teachers and students must be prepared when addressing conflict resolution.

Try This Out With Middle and Secondary Students

■ Peer mediation is a wonderful and effective strategy for helping students maintain their emotional balance, but peers and adult advisors need training. The important thing to remember is that educators must set the stage for conflict resolution by setting clear expectations for behavior. Teaching students the skills for managing anger appropriately comes next. Students need to know that anger is a normal emotion, and conflict is a part of life. Resilient students are not held hostage by their anger or emotions but learn to identify, understand, and deal effectively with them.

■ Be sure to allow students who are experiencing a conflict to cool off before moving to a room to try to iron out their issues in a mediation session. Remember, the brain and body are in an aroused state, and the rational mind is waiting in the wings.

■ Students need to get to the bottom of their emotions. Schools must make sure that students have access to trained counselors when necessary. Learning the intrapersonal skill of introspection will serve students long after graduation. Many adults in our society lack the ability to constructively second-guess themselves. They function on a surface level and never recognize or learn to deal with what lies underneath.

Consider This For All Students

■ In schools, it seems we most often attend to anger and angry behavior, but if someone could help students look deeper into their feelings, the anger often would look more like hurt or depression. Dealing with the primary feelings (hurt or depression) would most certainly help resolve the secondary emotion, anger. As the adults in charge of the climate of a school, we need to be careful not to be fooled by angry behavior. If we stop looking for the source of the behavior and simply respond with consequences, then no one has gained. The student becomes angrier and possibly more disruptive, and the school has not done its job of assisting students in knowing themselves and preparing for life. It is not always easy to work with angry youth. Sometimes, it takes months or years to build enough trust for students to respond to our efforts. The important thing is that we not give up but keep the resiliency attitude in mind. Each child has seeds of resilience within, so keep looking.

■ This is not a strategy, but it is something that a wise person told me. Whenever I feel myself getting discouraged, I find it very helpful. She said that we ought to allow one month of emotional recuperation for each year that a child has been experiencing difficulty either at home or at school. In other words, if you have an eighth-grade student who has been angry, disruptive, and unmotivated during the school career, allow that student 9 months to respond to your efforts. Of course, if this child was abused or neglected at a much younger age, then you may have to add some months. You see, educators think in school years, and time goes fast. We often try for a short time to help challenging kids but become discouraged when they reject our efforts. We can't understand when they do not appreciate the extra time and energy we give them. We seem to forget that we are asking many students to trust when they have learned not to trust, that trusting gets them hurt. We have to prove our commitment over time, because kids have been disappointed too often by adults who do not mean what they say or do not really care. We must not forget that the brain remembers feelings far better than it remembers facts. The key to reprogramming a student's behavior is patience and persistence in developing relationships in which trust and respect are prominent.

Summary

Possessing emotional literacy is an important key to success in life. Knowing and managing oneself, and having the ability to understand and empathize with others, are protective factors that assist all of us, especially those from high-risk environments. Schools are powerful places where students can learn about themselves in preparation for entry into the larger world. Educators hold privileged positions in that we create the environments in which students work and play. In truth, if educators attend to their students' emotional states, meaning that they allow opportunities for them to identify and express their feelings, solve problems, and resolve conflict, they will find that students are more capable of accessing their working memories and learning new information. Students will have greater chance for academic success when their socioemotional needs are addressed. Let's not waste the opportunity to assert our influence in the most resiliency-building ways possible.

5

Service Learning and Building Resilience

What I like best about participating in this group is that it is fun to work with the fourth graders. It was cool to be the teachers and explain to them how it is in fifth grade.

—Fifth-grade student who participated
in a transition to middle school program

I have loved service learning ever since I read essays written by fourth-grade, inner city kids about the experiences they had at the nursing home they visited. When I went to see for myself, I watched those kids as they arrived at the senior home, their faces excited because they knew the seniors were looking forward to their visit. I saw the transformation that happens when kids are allowed out of their school boundaries and offered opportunities to contribute in ways that are purely their own. I love watching what happens to kids when they are helping another. I think I love service learning so much because it is during service to others that the resilience inside

117

some of our students begins to shimmer. Sometimes, in a regular school setting, that same resilience is hidden behind layers of fear, academic failure, academic success, social stress, or social success. We often do not see the real student in the classroom setting. Sometimes we have to go into the real world and do real things to find the resilience that is in each of our kids.

Research on the impact of service learning reports positive changes in students who participate in service-learning projects. I was a believer in the power of service learning even before I read some of the research that supported my intuition. "Service learning programs may have the strongest evidence of any intervention that they reduced actual teen pregnancy rates while the youths are participating in the program (Kirby, 2001, pp. 13-14). Also, a nationwide survey of nearly 4,000 students involved in service learning programs revealed that about 75% reported learning "more" and "much more" in these courses than in those taught through traditional methods (Conrad & Hedin, 1991). Several reasons for these results are likely: participants develop relationships with program facilitators, they get a sense of autonomy and feelings of accomplishment, they feel more competent in their peer and adult relationships, and they are empowered by knowing that they can make a difference in another's life (Kirby, 2001). Whether we are trying to prevent pregnancy or engage students in commitment to school, I believe that service learning is a strategy that is effective. In addition, it incorporates all of the resiliency-building strategies that we have discussed so far.

Different Types of Service Learning

There are all types of service learning, and sometimes they can get confusing. It may help to focus on two different types. First, there is service learning that is curriculum related and second, there is service learning that is service related. Most programs combine both curriculum and service. Students who participate in service that is curriculum related may be asked to perform some service tasks that are related to particular subject matter being studied. As a result, they may retain subject content more easily and may see immediate application of subject material to the real world. Students who participate in service learning that is service related, or aimed solely at contributing to others in significant ways, gain self-confidence, life skills, and empathy. No matter how service learning is experienced, it is a powerful educational tool that can assist educators with their ultimate goal of preparing students for life.

Research tells us that resilient people have self-efficacy, strong relationships, autonomy, a sense of purpose, and the ability to solve problems (Benard, 1991). Through service learning experiences, students work on all these personal assets. One of the best things about service learning is that every student can participate and be successful. Well-planned service projects create opportunities for students to become participants, and they learn better in the process.

Service Was Once Part of Life

In the not so distant past, many youngsters worked on family farms or cared for siblings and elders or, in some other way, contributed to the survival of the family. In my own family, it was not uncommon for older children to work and pay toward family expenses. Before modern conveniences, life used to be much more difficult. Clothes dryers, washing machines, and vacuums only became common during the 1950s. There used to be many time-consuming chores to do, and youths were expected to pitch in. Today, with so many working parents and modern conveniences, many youths are no longer asked to help. Modern people have children for a variety of reasons but almost never because they *need* them for their ability to contribute. In fact, many families believe that the parents' job is to provide everything for their children and have stopped expecting any contribution in return. This seems to be the modern way, but our prosperity has come with a price. Many children are paying for the leisure and comfort they are given with their sense of self-efficacy and pride. For the most part, youths want to contribute in some way, but they need opportunities. Our youths are powerful resources with immense potential waiting to be tapped, and service learning is one way to do this. If we do not expect anything from our children, how can they learn to expect anything from themselves? It would be good to remember that Werner and Smith (1989) discovered that the resilient children of Kauai, Hawaii, were often the ones who were expected to contribute to the family's survival by working or caring for others. In that way, those children developed their competencies and bonded with their families.

Who Can Benefit From Service to Others?

It would be a mistake to think that impoverished youths from high-risk environments are less capable of contributing than their wealthier counterparts. They may not be asked or expected to give back because they have so little to begin with. It is demeaning to assume that young people who live in poverty would not want to help others or share their skills and talents. I have witnessed youngsters from the poverty of an inner city eagerly wait for their turns to go to deliver meals to elderly people. When asked to write about their experience, this is what one of these fourth-grade students said:

> When you go to the senior center it feels good because you make the seniors happy. It is very interesting talking to the seniors. They tell you about their life as a kid. It's fun serving the food because it's like you are a waiter at a restaurant. My mom tells me to be extra nice to seniors.

Young people learn quickly that, even if they have few material gifts to give, they can give of themselves.

A friend of mine who is a counselor in a suburban middle school convinced me of the power of service learning after she shared the following story. As part of an effort to engage her students in service to others, she took a group to the local soup kitchen to prepare and serve a meal. As a young woman filed through the food line, she recognized my friend. They shared a hug and spoke quietly for a few moments, much to the surprise and shock of her young students serving the food. Later, on the bus ride back to school, the students eagerly asked their counselor questions about the woman. They wanted to know how she knew someone who needed a meal from a soup kitchen.

They were surprised to learn that the two had been in the same high school class. Unfortunately, this woman had made some bad decisions in life, including the decision to use drugs and alcohol. The students and counselor then had a realistic discussion about making decisions and living with their consequences. The students shared reflections of some of their own decisions. This was one of those rare teachable moments. There is little or no chance for most students to *witness* the long-term consequences of poor decisions in the classroom. However, in this instance, the students could see and immediately apply their new learning because they were present for this real-life encounter. My friend assured me that 100 lessons on decision making could never have taught those students what their experience taught that day. After hearing this story, I was hooked on the potential inherent in service learning, and I wanted to know more.

In my search for information about service learning, I soon discovered that there are many interpretations and definitions. Some schools are calling their high school requirement for community service service learning. Others are interpreting the definition much more literally, and consider only those activities that are tied directly to the classroom curriculum to be service learning. Most fall somewhere in between. Some states, such as Maryland, are way ahead with their service learning because the educational leaders in their system have made it a priority. Other states lag far behind (Boston, 1997). This chapter will provide a brief history of the origins of service learning, attempt to clear up the confusion about different types of service learning, present the concept of a continuum of service learning, and explain its relationship to building resiliency in students.

We have talked about using the resiliency wheel as a guide to develop strategies for implementing the concepts and theories addressed in this book. Service learning itself is inherent in all parts of the resiliency wheel. In addition, we will see how many elements of good educational practice, such as multiple intelligences, performance-based assessment, emotional intelligence, and character education are all enhanced through service learning.

ORIGINS OF THE CONCEPT OF SERVICE LEARNING

There is a lot of truth to the statement, "Everything old is new again." Just as with character education, the seeds of service learning were planted by one of our early 20th-century educational leaders, John Dewey. "Many contemporary practitioners continue to see service learning as an attempt to carry out Dewey's program for educational and social reform" (Tai-Seale, 2000, p. 256). "John Dewey suggested that we learn primarily through experience and need community-based learning to understand how to practice citizen skills in a democracy" (Shumer, 2000, p. 34). The term *service learning* began, almost unnoticed, in the 1960s and began developing rapidly in the 1980s. It is both a practice and a philosophy of education which began with Dewey and was elaborated on by two other notable educators, Kolb and Freire (Tai-Seale, 2000).

The three important seeds planted by Dewey that are woven through all types of service learning to varying degrees are

- Students should learn through an experiential engagement with society that should progress toward performing conscious acts of social service.
- Reflection on experience is key to understanding.
- Reciprocal learning occurs for both students and teachers during the process. (Tai-Seale, 2000)

What Is Service Learning?

Currently, there are many definitions of service learning. For example: "Any carefully monitored service experience in which a student has intentional learning goals and reflects actively on what he or she is learning throughout the experience" (National Society of Experiential Education cited in Billig, 2000, p. 659). A general definition is this: a method under which students learn and develop through active participation in thoughtfully organized service that is conducted in, and meets the needs of, a community; is coordinated with a school or community service program; helps foster civic responsibility; is integrated into and enhances the core curriculum of the students; and provides structured time for reflection (Billig, 2000). For the 1999 National Student Service Learning and Community Service Survey conducted by the U.S. Department of Education, service learning was defined as

Curriculum-based community service that integrates classroom instruction with community service activities. The service must: be organized in relation to an academic course or curriculum, have clearly stated learning objectives, address real community needs in a sustained manner over a period of time, and assist students in drawing lessons from the service through regularly scheduled, organized reflection or critical analysis activities, such as classroom discussions, presentation, or directed writing. (Westat, 1999, p. 3)

Prevalence of Service Learning

The U.S. Department of Education survey provided the first reliable estimates of the percentage of schools incorporating service learning into their curriculum as well as providing the most recent data on school engagement in community service. This is what they found:

- 64% of all public schools, including 83% of public high schools, had students participating in community service activities recognized or arranged by the school.

- 57% of all public schools organized community service activities for their students.

- 32% of all public schools organized service learning as part of their curriculum, including half of all high schools. (Westat, 1999)

It is clear from this survey that service learning is becoming more prevalent in American schools. "In 1984, just 27 percent of all high schools reported having community service and 9 percent reported having service learning (Billig, 2000, p. 659). During the 1998-to-1999 school year, these percentages were 83 percent and 46 percent respectively" (Westat, 1999, p. 12). These statistics, while encouraging, are still confusing. It is not entirely clear what schools mean when they report that they are involving students in service learning. We are left wondering to what degree the students are involved and what the quality of the service-learning experience is. In my experience, most educators are left to their own devices when implementing service-learning strategies. According to the 1999 survey, 83% of teachers received support, but when the numbers are broken down, that support is not usually long term or systemic. For example, only 15% of teachers received extra planning time for service learning activities, only 11% received a reduction in course load, only 3% were hired as full-time service-learning coordinators (Westat, 1999, p. 9).

In other words, teachers or counselors do most service learning as part of, or in addition to, their regular duties. If that is the case, and they choose to continue, then they must definitely believe in its value because, depending on the type of service, service learning can come with plenty of additional preparation and organization. However, all the extra work seems to be well worth it. Research done on the impact of service learning in seven middle and ten high schools in nine states by Brandeis University's Center for Human Resources and Abt Associates indicates that well-designed service learning has very positive effects. These researchers studied over 300 Learn and Serve America projects and found that they had a positive impact on civic development of participants as well as on personal and social responsibility, acceptance of diversity, educational engagement and achievement, and service leadership (Melchior, 1999).

Service Learning Benefits

A summary of research on K-12, school-based service learning finds the following positive effects of engaging students in service-learning projects:

- Students who participate are less likely to engage in risky behaviors.
- Service learning has a positive effect on students' interpersonal development and ability to relate to culturally diverse groups.
- Service learning helps develop students' sense of civic responsibility and citizenship skills.
- Service learning helps students acquire academic skills and knowledge.
- Students who participate in service learning are more engaged with their studies and more motivated to learn.
- Service learning is associated with increased attendance.
- Service learning helps students become more realistic about careers.
- Service learning results in greater mutual respect between teachers and students.
- Service learning leads to more positive perceptions of school and youths on the part of community members. (Billig, 2000)

CONFUSION SURROUNDING SERVICE LEARNING

Even with the definitions available, service learning means different things to different people. Some view it very broadly, believing that any service done by a student in the community is service learning. Others believe that only curriculum-related service ought to be considered service learning. However it is defined, the one factor that separates service learning from community service is the opportunity for reflection. "Reflection may take place through guided discussions, debates, group presentations, journal writing, or the dialogue journal in which conversations take place between a student and teacher, mentor, or other adult" (Boston, 1997, p. 5).

All types of service learning have great merit and positive benefits for kids. Some strategies are quite simple, others can become complicated and time consuming. Students reap huge benefits from even the most simple service projects. It is important that educators do not get too stuck on following a definition to the letter, because that trepidation may mean they will not try any service projects at all. That would be a terrible loss. Sometimes, projects involve direct service, and, sometimes, they involve contributing in more general ways. The best part is that students from affluent backgrounds as well as students from economically deprived backgrounds can give to others who are less fortunate or use their talents and energy to contribute and learn in the process. No matter how impoverished people are, if they can assist another or give of themselves in some way, they feel richer. After service learning experiences, young people often talk about how good it feels to help others. By contributing in meaningful ways, students build self-esteem and self-efficacy. Very often, those with the fewest material assets are the ones who will benefit the most from giving of themselves.

Your Goals Drive Your Service Learning

Most of my experience with service learning has been via counselors who provide students with opportunities to contribute in meaningful ways. They often are working with marginal students who are not very engaged in their learning for a wide variety of personal, family, social, or academic reasons. Their objective is to get kids involved in acts of contribution or service with the goal of increasing their motivation to learn, increasing their acquisition of social skills, and increasing their bonding to both the school and community. Their goal drives the type of service learning they choose to engage in.

When beginning a service-learning project, it is most helpful to establish whether your primary goal is to provide service from which students learn broad life lessons such as self-confidence, interpersonal skills, social responsibility, and citizenship, or whether your goal is to provide specific learning that is enhanced through service. A learning-first approach means the service is determined by the academic content of the curriculum (Tai-Seale, 2000). A service-focused approach has almost unlimited possibilities. A learning-focused approach must make sure that the service is related to the learning. For example, students learning about social and economic effects of pollution might clean up local parks and research the cost of cleaning up others' trash. The service is an enhancement of the course content. On the other hand, students who wish to clean up local parks purely as a contribution might focus, during reflection, on their own feelings related to making their community a better place to be. They might also reflect on working as a member of a team effort or, possibly, reflect on relevant social issues. I am hopeful that this perspective will clear up some confusion and does not place a value judgment on which approach is better. Rather, it allows the goal to drive the process.

An Example of a Learning-Focused Approach

I am aware of a teacher who uses service learning as part of a yearlong project in her seventh-grade English class. She requires students to choose a topic "worthy of their attention" that they focus on throughout the entire year. Grammar, reading, writing, and speaking skills are taught through the topics that each student chooses. Students choose topics that they want to know more about, such as drug addiction, pollution, having to wear bike helmets, and so forth. They are free to choose a topic, with teacher approval, as long as it is worthy of their yearlong attention. Throughout the year, the students do research, and the teacher monitors progress by using benchmarks. In addition, the students are required to do service related to their topic.

I learned of this teacher from one of her students, a young man from her class who presented at a conference on service learning. As his yearlong topic, he decided to study head trauma because he was frustrated that his mother made him wear a bike helmet. He was sure he would find out that they were useless, and then he would be off the hook. He arranged to do his service at the head trauma unit at a local hospital. As it turned out, he learned to appreciate the reasons behind his mom's concern.

During his presentation, he very eloquently explained his topic, the research on bike injuries, his gradual change in attitude, and so forth. As he concluded, he said something that I will always remember. He said, "The difference between me and a kid who doesn't wear a helmet is that I have a brain." Clearly, his experience left a deep impression on him. What a wonderful way for this student to learn how to do research, to write a report, to speak in front of a group, and to understand the benefit of wearing a helmet to protect such a valuable resource. Seeing and assisting other young people who suffered injuries solidified the learning and made him appreciate his mother's concern. It seems to me that any extra work this teacher did was well worth it.

This student, and all of this teacher's students, benefited from having choice and responsibility for their learning. Students were free to choose their topics, had flexibility and choice in their approach, and presented their information according to their preferred styles. They were actively engaged and motivated. In addition, their contributing to others as part of service helped them build empathy and character as well as confidence and self-awareness. It is clear that this approach incorporates all of the resiliency-building concepts we have covered so far in this book.

An Example of a Service-Focused Approach

Four counselors in a local district developed a program to ease the transition from elementary to middle school. This program has been operating for the past 8 years with wonderful results. In addition to assisting students in transition, the primary goal of the program is to create an opportunity for the middle school students to participate actively in making a meaningful contribution to the school. This goal, and many more equally important ones, are achieved through this program. The program is considered a form of peer leadership.

The first year of the program, the counselors surveyed all fourth graders to determine what their biggest concerns were regarding moving to the middle school. They found that the fourth graders were very worried about opening lockers, doing homework, finding bathrooms, getting in trouble, escaping bullies, and so forth. Next, the counselors took these concerns to the fifth graders at the middle school and asked them what they thought they could do to help the younger kids feel better about coming to their school. The fifth graders easily recalled their own fears about moving into the middle school. They were the pioneers of this program and created the program's structure, which remains today.

To start, all fourth and fifth graders got a pen pal buddy. Letters of introduction were sent back and forth. The fifth graders then began helping to plan the day at the end of the year when the fourth graders would be bussed to the middle school. They set up stations on various topics where groups of younger students listen to older students tell them what to expect. Stations had to do with homework, cafeteria routines, rules and in-school suspension, and so forth. One station had to do with opening lockers, where the fifth graders took the fourth graders to their lockers and taught them how to use the combinations. Tours of the school were given, and friendships, or at least acquaintances, were made. Subsequent fifth graders remember their own fears and think about how the program helped them. They are eager to repay the kindness and become the helper instead of the helped.

This day does far more than help fourth graders feel comfortable. The fifth-grade students develop empathy, organization skills, appreciation for working within a system, and, most important, a feeling of pride and accomplishment that only comes from helping another. Additionally, when the new fifth graders arrive the next fall, they already know an older buddy. The climate of the school is positively affected by this familiarity. This service-focused approach achieves its goals. Fourth graders make a better transition, and fifth graders contribute in a meaningful way. Quite possibly, the older students get the most from the experience. This is a quote from a fifth-grade student:

> What I liked best about participating in this group was to have six little faces paying attention to me. It made me feel so responsible to know I was filling their heads (with) knowledge. I (sic) made me feel like I was a real teacher.

In this service-focused approach, students' active engagement leads to motivation and school engagement. Pen pal letters written as part of language arts have meaning because they are real, and they will be answered. In addition, contributing to such an important effort leads to confidence, empathy, and self-esteem. Service learning can have very positive benefits for school climate.

THE CONTINUUM OF SERVICE LEARNING

Considering service learning from the service-focused and the learning-focused perspectives simplifies things immensely. Even so, there are many ways to implement service learning, some more complicated than others. Indirect service is fairly simple, while direct service is often accompanied by additional organizational tasks. Busy educators may unnecessarily shy away from all service learning because they do not understand the continuum concept (Figure 5.1). By thinking of indirect-service projects on the left side of a continuum and

Figure 5.1   Service Learning Continuum

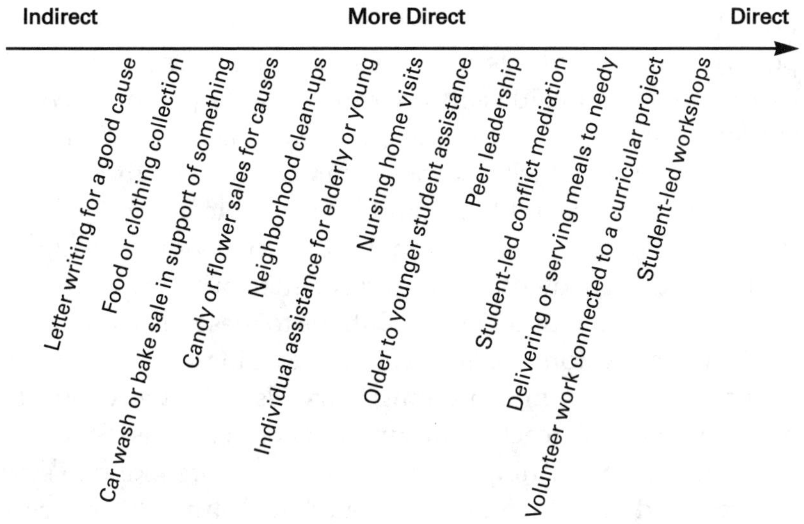

Indirect   More Direct   Direct

Letter writing for a good cause
Food or clothing collection
Car wash or bake sale in support of something
Candy or flower sales for causes
Neighborhood clean-ups
Individual assistance for elderly or young
Nursing home visits
Older to younger student assistance
Peer leadership
Student-led conflict mediation
Delivering or serving meals to needy
Volunteer work connected to a curricular project
Student-led workshops

direct service projects on the right side, it is easier to determine which activities best suit your needs and your ability to implement them effectively. Engaging students in simple actions such as writing letters to legislators in support of worthy causes or collecting canned goods for food pantries are among the least labor-intensive activities for educators. These activities are considered service learning and can easily be tied to curricular content in language arts, math, or social studies. Moving along the continuum, activities become more active, and therefore, more complicated to organize and sustain.

Using the Continuum

Figure 5.1 illustrates very simple examples of service learning (left side) and moves toward more labor-intensive examples (right side). Educators can easily integrate some simple service into course content and require students to write, discuss, or speak about their experiences as they relate to their subject matter. For example, students learning about the Depression may be asked to collect food and make contributions to nonprofit food pantries as a way to understand that poverty remains with us and that social structures are set up to assist people today, 70 years after the Great Depression. While stocking pantries, students may be required as part of their service learning to gather statistics regarding how many families use food pantries, and this could be related to economics and the reality of the working poor. Not only would students understand their own communities better but they also may begin thinking about possible solutions to these issues.

When educators see that service learning can take many forms, it may seem more inviting to try. Usually, the benefits to both student and teacher are immediately obvious. Students who can attach meaning to their work are more likely to stay focused and remain more motivated to learn. This success benefits teachers as well as students. As time goes on, teachers may wish to incorporate more service learning activities routinely. As educators begin to incorporate service learning into their plans, some changes may occur. Teachers may begin to move away from being the center point of the classroom and move toward being a coach who helps students find and nurture their own potential. To do this, teachers would have to possess the resiliency attitude that allows them to believe in all students' ability to take responsibility for their own learning.

The major tasks that accompany direct service learning have to do with organization and recruitment of project allies, such as principals, parents, other educators, and community contacts. Establishing community relationships, organizing transportation, getting permission slips, and coordinating schedules are a few of the tasks that usually need to be done. Though time consuming, these are fairly simple. The harder part is that teachers who really wish to become coaches instead of lecturers must let go of absolute control of the curriculum content and, instead, offer a framework on which students can build according to interest. In learning-focused service, students

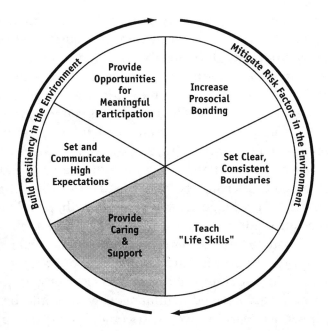

gradually assume more control for their learning, usually at the middle or high school level. Students become empowered participants in their learning instead of passive receptacles.

The additional work associated with service learning may be daunting when educators are faced with so many other responsibilities. That is why starting on the left side of the continuum is a good idea. If an educator chooses to move forward on the continuum, it would be helpful to get assistance from counselors, parents, and other interested parties to plan and implement the more time-consuming service learning activities. One little warning: Once students get a taste of learning like this, they will want more of it.

SERVICE LEARNING AND BUILDING RESILIENCE

As I said earlier in this chapter, service learning is related to all six elements of the resiliency wheel. It is a strategy as well as a concept that builds assets in students and enhances their ability to be resilient. If you refer to the Search Institute's (1997)

40 Assets in Figure 1.5, you may easily see that service learning is connected to *empowerment* of youths. Through their service and contribution, youths come to be valued by their communities and are given useful roles. Service learning is connected to *educational commitment* in that the student is actively engaged in learning and is motivated to do well. It is connected to *values* in that the youths place a high value on helping other people, promoting equality, and taking responsibility. It is related to *social competencies* in that youths develop planning skills as well as empathy, sensitivity, and friendship skills. Students often acquire knowledge of, and comfort with, people of different backgrounds. Service learning is related to *positive identity* in that youths have better self-esteem, an internal locus of control, a purpose in life, and optimism about their futures. The most amazing thing about service learning is that so many benefits are derived simultaneously. It would be wonderful if service learning would become a consistent part of every child's school experience.

WORKING THE WHEEL

We have talked about ideas for service learning projects earlier in this chapter. There are as many possibilities for projects as one can imagine. Rather than offering specific Try-This-Out suggestions for each part of the wheel, as we have done in previous chapters, I will, instead, connect the segments of the wheel to the rationale for service learning.

Provide Caring and Support

Through service learning, students learn to give care and support as well as receive it. Many projects involve assisting elders, younger students, peers, less fortunate people, physically or mentally challenged people, animals, and so forth. Through assisting and caring for others, students actually care for themselves. The old adage that the more one gives, the more one receives in return is true. This paradox is surprising for students who have never been asked or provided with opportunities to contribute to others in meaningful ways. Yet these students are quick to express how good it feels to help others, and they really get it that giving of yourself makes you richer in the best ways. Counselors have reported to me that the most disruptive students in school become the most gentle and caring when working with elders or younger children. It is almost as if they are giving what they wish someone would give them. Unless they have opportunities to give in service to others, we, and they, may never know what internal character they possess and what they have to offer another person or a community.

Set and Communicate High Expectations

It is great to have high expectations for students, but only if the appropriate resources and support exist for them to be successful in meeting those expectations. Service learning, because of its utility in enhancing learning and retention, is a strategy that is useful to educators who have high expectations for their students. Students learn best when they are emotionally connected to their subject content, and when they see purpose and meaning for what they are learning. That is why service learning has such potential for bringing schoolwork to life. Service connects learning with real life. "Service learning provides a means to integrate school subjects with real-world settings" (Boston, 1997, p. 4).

Provide Opportunities for Meaningful Participation

This part of the wheel is, of course, the most obviously connected to service. Service learning is the most sophisticated version of helping. It is beyond having chores or duties assigned to students, because it incorporates structure, opportunity for reflection, and connection to learning. Creative educators have almost unlimited opportunities to devise ways for kids to contribute to the smooth operation of the school or classroom. Usually, students are eager to get involved once they trust that their thoughts and opinions will be taken seriously. Too often, we ignore this incredible resource and then wonder why students seem unmotivated or disenfranchised. Very often, the most unmotivated students are the ones we ought to be engaging in service learning projects.

Increase Prosocial Bonding

Students who have opportunities to work together as teams, or to see one another outside the traditional classroom structure, often learn to appreciate the traits and talents that make each one of them unique. Service learning projects provide interactive opportunities for students to make and carry out decisions. It is okay to talk, laugh, argue and resolve conflict, and be authentic. Students may feel more bonded to school and, possibly, make new friendships in the process.

Set Clear and Consistent Boundaries

Before any students enter a situation in which they will be offering a service, there is much groundwork to be laid. Students need to understand what to expect, what the service recipients need, what rules exist, what dress is appropriate, what level of conduct is acceptable, what will happen if they are not able to comply with the rules and procedures, and so forth. This preparation is important for students' success. The best part about these ground rules is that, once again, they are based in reality, and students can immediately understand the reasons for them. They begin to realize that a school principal must plan ahead when allowing students out of class for a trip. They see that busses do not just appear but that someone has to request and pay for them. They see that permission slips are necessary so that students' whereabouts are accounted for, and parents are involved in the decision. They also recognize the need for appropriate behavior and usually rise to the level of expectation set for them.

Teach Life Skills

Students acquire many life skills through service learning projects, including conflict resolution, decision-making, problem-solving, and communication skills; self-awareness;

appreciation for diversity; an understanding of the rules and regulations that govern systems; organizational skills; civic pride; and community understanding. The best part is that they acquire these skills in an authentic way rather than artificially. As my counselor friend realized when her students saw a person whom their teacher knew suffering the consequences of bad decisions, relying on classroom instruction to learn how to make good decisions seemed ridiculous. The impact of their first-hand experience that day would far outweigh any lesson plan. The same could be said of most life skills. Out of context, they are difficult to grasp and apply. As we know from character education, life skills are better lived than taught.

Try This Out With All Ages

■ **Create a Peace Corps in your school or classroom.** No matter what grade level you work with, ask your students what they think could be better about their school. Ask them to write an answer to a question from brief solution-oriented therapy (see Chapter 1) such as, "If you woke up tomorrow and came to school, and it was just as you dreamed it would be, what would be different?" They may say things relating to cafeteria food, cafeteria behavior, litter, students' behavior toward one another, teachers, discipline, and so forth. It doesn't matter how they answer. It only matters that you listen, record responses, and discuss their thoughts with them. It would be best to keep responses anonymous. You could compile the ideas and then share them as a group so that everyone can react, relate, and choose one or two. Then, enlist their help in working on these throughout the year.

■ **Become the facilitator of ideas.** Be the person to ask for students' help. Provide the opportunity for kids to contribute, and provide the resources that students might need to do so. You are the person who has the knowledge that they don't have, so help guide them. Sometimes kids are aware of problems that we have not yet seen, and they may think of solutions that we might never have thought of. Be careful not to unconsciously set up roadblocks. Let them try new ideas as long as they are safe. You may have to let them learn through trial and error. You may think that some will never work, and you might be surprised.

SUMMARY

Close your eyes and see if you can remember a very positive experience from your own school years. Got one? I suspect that the experience you recalled has something to do with an accomplishment of yours. I also suspect that it had something to do with how you felt when you had something of value to offer and your contribution was recognized. I imagine that it also was a time when you were actively involved in something rather than sitting at a desk. If I am correct, then you know how good it feels to be engaged in your learning and recognized for doing something meaningful. It would be great to help recreate that feeling for today's students, don't you think?

Increasing evidence suggests that service learning is a strategy with enormous potential to enhance the learning of all students, from the most motivated to the most disruptive and disenfranchised. It is a character-building, resiliency-building, asset-building strategy that incorporates multiple intelligences and emotional literacy. Most of all, it is a way for teachers to liven up dry subject matter and engage even reluctant students in their learning. "It is not icing on the educational cake but vital to learning" (Boston, 1997, p. 5).

With so much already on their plates, teachers may be reluctant to try to incorporate service learning into their curriculum and pedagogy. For those willing to give it a try, starting small is a good idea. Work ideas from the left side of the continuum into your plans and gradually build in more, moving right. Let your goal drive your process. Do you want to enhance your subject matter? Do you want to offer disruptive children an opportunity to show their true self? Is there a child who just isn't interested in anything? Possibly getting that child involved in service of some kind will light a spark. Maybe one service project per year would be a prudent way to start. Service learning can take place at any grade level, with all types of students. Whatever extra time and energy it takes to implement, the payoff will be well worth it. Watch out, though, the kids are going to love it!

6

Violence Prevention and Building Resilience

No magic solution exists. We will not develop one project that will eliminate hate and prejudice or end violence, but we can begin to change the culture in which the use of degrading language and violence appears acceptable to our students.

—Stephen Wessler (2000/2001, p. 31)

It is no accident that this chapter is at the end of the book. In many ways, it is a fitting summary of all that we have just talked about. The strategies so far offered are avenues to empowering students by engaging them in their learning, assisting them in knowing and managing themselves successfully, and helping them to build their characters through assets that they can use to navigate the world. We have discussed how students who can identify and successfully manage their feelings are less susceptible to passion and emotions. We understand that schools that focus on creating climates where every student is respected and protected are less likely to miss the signs of low-level violence that can escalate into physical violence. This book is all about helping educators see that they are the ones who create school environments that can either promote or discourage young peoples' growth. Many of you are already using many of the strategies we have mentioned. I am sure that many of you feel like lone wolves and wish that everyone in your school would get on the same page. Your instincts are correct. Resiliency-building schools, in fact, do have staff members who operate from a common belief system.

Too often, legislators, media, and parents turn their attention to schools only in response to negative incidents. Low test scores, fighting, unpopular decisions, or gun violence attract many eyes. A great deal of attention is paid to violence in schools. As a result of media coverage of shootings in Mississippi, Oregon, California, Arkansas, and Colorado from 1997 through 2000, we hear disturbing statistics such as

> During the 1996-to-1997 school year, 47% of all public schools reported to police the occurrence of at least one less-serious violent crime (physical attack or fight without a weapon) or nonviolent crime (theft or vandalism), and an additional 10% reported at least one serious violent crime. (Mitchell, 2000, p. 2)

Articles emerge daily with perspectives on what is wrong with our youths and what we can do to them and for them to stop the violence. Well-meaning people want safety immediately, so they advocate for quick fixes like locker searches, metal detectors, harsh punishments, and stronger policies. Sadly, as in the case of Columbine or Santana high schools, high-level violence is drawing this intense attention when it is too late to help either the victims or the victimizers. Why aren't more people questioning the environments that these acts of violence occurred within? Many people needed to pay attention sooner. Schools need to address the low-level violence effectively if they wish to avoid these tragedies. If they don't, everyone will have the potential to become a victim, including the shooters themselves. Metal detectors are no protection for the type of violence that most of the shooters suffered long before they picked up a gun. I believe that killing another is horrific, and it cannot be excused. It can, however, be analyzed and better understood. If we are to prevent other tragedies like these, we had better remedy the fact that many people missed, and continue to miss, the signs of low-level violence that may eventually lead to murder.

Students are victims in systems where benign neglect is the norm. Some educators may be enabling violent behavior and not even realize it. One reason for this is because each person in a school setting may understand violence differently. Unless everyone is in agreement with a consistent definition of violence, and in agreement with a definite response to it via policies and procedures, many students will be enabled to continue unchecked, inappropriate behavior. The most effective approaches to curbing school violence start with a definition of violent behavior that all staff members accept, for example: "Violence is any word, look, sign, or act that hurts a person's body, feelings, or things" (Hazelden, 1999, p. 31).

When educators and support staff in a school do not have this basis for understanding, it is very difficult to create an environment where all staff members enforce consequences for inappropriate behavior in a consistent, fair way before it escalates into more serious behavior.

Violence starts long before guns are brought to school, often with gossip and dirty looks. Kids who are different are singled out and made to feel self-conscious and bad about themselves. Adults may not notice, or they may think that this behavior, although unfortunate, is normal. Most of the time, adults do not realize that this behavior is a form of violence. More than likely, educators may feel ill-equipped to deal with low-level violence. They secretly dislike the "mean" kids and root for the "good" kids but still do little to change the situation. After all, they think, how can one person make a difference in an adolescent culture like this? Enabling violence is composed of the misguided beliefs, feelings, attitudes, and actions that allow the negative behavior to continue (Remboldt, 1998). Some of those beliefs may include the following: your intervention will have little effect; the behavior is somehow normal; if you intervene, you will lose popularity among students; or if you intervene, you will not be supported by your administration. Sometimes these beliefs have a basis in reality, unfortunately. That is why administrators must ensure that clear, consistent policies are going to be backed up with consequences that they will support in every instance, even with athletes and other students who enjoy elevated status in a school setting.

In response to the tragic shootings over the past few years, many schools in my area have begun to implement programs designed to address the issue of violence in our schools. A violence prevention framework from Hazelden (1999) titled Respect and Protect, and its curriculum counterpart, the No-Bullying Program (Bitney & Title, 2001), are programs employing a whole-school approach. I had the opportunity to observe a lesson from this program being taught to a third-grade class. The topic that day had to do with empowering students to use their eyes and ears to assist other children who are being bullied. As an example, the teacher stressed that, even if an adult is not nearby, when students see another being bullied, they could find a friend or two and approach the bully to say that they think what the bully is doing is wrong. The students practiced doing this through role-plays until they became reasonably comfortable with the appropriate words to use. At the end of the lesson, the teacher asked this simple question: "Isn't it about time that all this bullying stopped?" The class erupted into applause and cheers. I have observed many lessons in my time as an administrator, but that was the first time that I ever saw children applaud at the end. I had the distinct feeling that these children were very much relieved that someone, especially their teacher, was finally helping them with an all-too-familiar problem.

Educators need support to be able to assert themselves in a school culture, especially at the middle and high school levels. My sister, who has taught eighth grade for many years, recalls a painful story. Her principal created a rule that no one could eat in hallways because new carpet had been installed. My sister sent two girls to see him because she found them eating cookies at their lockers. The only thing that happened as a result of her enforcing the rule was that the girls disliked her for being mean. The principal had not done his homework. He asked his staff to enforce a rule that seemed logical, but he did not have logical consequences in mind for someone who broke the rule. He let the girls go with an admonition not to eat in the hallways, rather than asking them to do something logical, such as vacuum or sweep up the hall that day. My sister felt unsupported and was discouraged from observing any further infractions of that rule. The stakes are, however, much higher when it comes to observing acts of low-level violence. Principals must support their staffs when they enforce agreed-on rules.

Educators and support staff, when they do not feel capable of generating an effective response, when they feel that their efforts will not have an impact, or when they fear that they will not be supported by administration, may pretend not to see a violent action of a student. Staff may feel that a child is too far out of control and be intimidated. They may give a disapproving look but do nothing about the behavior. Others may excuse or rationalize the behavior of a student, even suggesting that another student provoked the incident. Some do not know the procedures for reporting an incident and fear being perceived by the administration as finding problems. All these obstacles work together to promote a climate where low-level violence can flourish. Without a clear definition of violence and clear policies and procedures to follow when an incident is noted, staff members will unwittingly enable low-level violent behavior.

Benard (1991) says that the home, school, and community need to work together for the benefit of our kids. But communities, local and global, vary in their responses to the problem of youth violence. Earlier in this book, I expressed the belief that too often, educators seem to be carrying a heavier load than either home or communities when it comes to preparing young people for their futures. This last chapter will be no exception. It has been my experience that some programs of a recreational nature are available for youths in certain communities, but few, if any, programs exist in the community where youths can acquire personal skills for nonviolence. If they do, they are usually attached to family court or probation. They reach a limited population of youths. Likewise, homes and families vary in their abilities to instruct their children in emotional literacy and nonviolent interactions. It is common for parents to lack understanding of all the different forms of violence and their impact on their children. That brings us back to schools and educators.

Educators can directly affect the school environments of which they are a part and help to create. They usually have little or no ability to change families or communities, but their power within the school is immense. They are role models, and through their example and instruction, children may learn how to handle, or even intervene in, low-level violence situations. It takes courage to take a stand against low-level violence, and students become empowered with this courage when they see their teachers willing to do so (Wessler, 2000/2001).

In many ways, schools are the most predictable, safest places that many students know. Students congregate, interact, learn, and grow within their walls. For most kids, any pain associated with school is taken in stride, and they emerge no worse for the experience. For many, however, school can be a stressful, life-altering experience because of the emotional toll that negative school experiences exact. Wallach says, "The awareness, threat, or experience of school violence can result in a growing sense of fear, and fear erodes the academic environment. Children who continuously expend energy to defend themselves against real or imagined dangers have difficulty learning" (cited in Mitchell, 2000, p. 3). As I said, the heaviest load rests with the schools because educators have (or can acquire) the ability to create the environments and teach the skills that kids need to lead productive, nonviolent lives.

UNDERSTANDING LOW-LEVEL VIOLENCE

It seems that the common thread among all the recent school shootings is that all the students who shot others had been bullied. They had been victims of psychological intimidation and harassment for many years before resorting to gun violence. Not all victims of low-level violence become murderers. If they did, we'd have daily killings. School shootings are a rare occurrence, but low-level violence in our schools is rampant. Most students suffer in silence. Other victims often fear school and stay home rather than face more humiliation and intimidation. Seven percent of American eighth graders stay home one time per month because of bullies (Banks, 2000). Unfortunately, many students do not think that educators would or could do anything to stop their plight. Most victims do not even tell their parents. "Student surveys reveal that only a small percentage of students seem to believe that adults will help. Students feel that adult intervention is infrequent and ineffective and that telling adults will only bring more harassment from bullies" (Banks, 2000, p. 13). Sadly, educators often view low-level violence, which includes teasing, gossip, dirty looks, ostracism, and bullying, as normal rites of passage and often do not intervene until it has escalated into fist fights or theft (Banks, 2000). School administrators and teachers often underreact to low-level violence, and this type of verbal and emotional abuse can leave painful scars. It is hard to hide physical wounds, but emotional wounds can fester, deeply hidden, until it is too late (Brill, 2000b).

Where Does It Start?

It is important for educators to understand that, usually, physical violence is a culmination of events, not a precipitating event. Sometimes, the person who gets caught hitting is the one who was being picked on in the first place. Remember that the definition of violence includes words, looks, and acts. If one had a continuum for violent behavior, the low-level side would start on the left and might include gossip, leering, ostracizing, and gesturing, and the middle to the right side would include higher-level violence such as verbal abuse, tripping, shoving, hitting, and so forth.

Students exist and interact in a culture that often goes unnoticed by the educators in a school. While teachers focus on their lessons and do their best to motivate and engage students in their learning, students are often interacting in negative, less obvious ways. As I recall my own school experience, everyone knew who was smart, who was dangerous, who was popular, who was not, and who was to be avoided. All of us instinctively knew the difference between peer violence and bullying. Peer violence is conflict between two or more individuals who are equally matched in power and stems from arguments or misunderstandings. Bullying is repeated, intentionally harmful behavior between people who are not of equal strength, stature, resources, or power (Bitney & Title, 2001). Students know who is being bullied and who are the bullies. Very often, students will avoid the victims who are being picked on, not because they do not like them but because they are afraid to lose status by associating with them, and they do not want to increase their own chances for being bullied (Banks, 2000). Educators may notice that some students seem isolated, quiet, and withdrawn. They may worry about them or even try to help them. But the reality is that if students are being bullied, chances are excellent that the educator will not hear it from them. Educators must tune in to the subculture and become alert to signs and indications of low-level aggression among students.

Who Gets Bullied and Who Does the Bullying?

The first researcher to focus on bullying behavior was Olweus from Norway. He, and others after him, discovered

---

Box 6.1

CHARACTERISTICS OF BULLIES

- Need to feel powerful and in control
- Enjoy inflicting suffering on victims
- Have little empathy, often blame the victims
- Often come from homes with excessive physical punishment
- Lack of parental warmth and involvement
- Defiant toward adults
- Antisocial
- Break school rules
- Have little anxiety
- Have strong self-esteem
- Can successfully hide their behavior
- Average students
- Small circle of friends
- Impulsive
- Interpret ambiguous acts as hostile

SOURCE: Banks, 2000; Hazelden Foundation, 1999.

---

common characteristics of those who bully and their victims through extensive study of school incidents (Banks, 2000; Hazelden, 1999). The characteristics noted for bullies are listed in Box 6.1.

Similarly, there are certain characteristics that are common to victims. These are listed in Box 6.2.

As we view these lists, no doubt we can remember students from our own classroom experiences who fit those descriptions.

Box 6.2

CHARACTERISTICS OF PASSIVE VICTIMS

- Anxious, insecure and cautious
- Have low self-esteem
- Rarely retaliate or defend themselves
- Lack social skills, friends and often are socially isolated
- Close to their parents; may be overprotected by parents
- Physically weaker than their peers
- Rarely tell because they think it will make matters worse
- Sensitive and cry easily
- May carry weapons for self-protection
- Do not invite attack

SOURCE: Banks, 2000; Hazelden Foundation, 1999.

It has been my experience that almost everyone can recall a person who was singled out and picked on, and almost everyone can recall the kids who picked on them. It seems that things have not changed for the better but, rather, have gotten worse. In Hazelden's No-Bullying Program (Bitney & Title, 2001), there is a distinction made between passive victims and provocative victims. Provocative victims are often perceived as those students who bring their problems on themselves. Very often, teachers and other staff members find it difficult to feel sorry for them because their behavior may be annoying to them, as well. These victims suffer greatly because they are most likely acting out in various ways (dressing differently, taking unpopular stances on issues, acting silly, calling

Box 6.3

CHARACTERISTICS OF PROVOCATIVE VICTIMS

- Pester and irritate others

- Quick tempered and will fight back

- Get others upset

- Can look like a bully, but is always a victim

- Clumsy, immature, restless

- Provoke attacks

- Isolated

- Friendless

- Overly dependent on adults

- Distressed

- May be learning disabled

- May have ADD or ADHD

- Are bullied repeatedly

SOURCE: From *Respect and Protect Violence Prevention and Intervention*, p. 32. Copyright © 1999 by Hazelden Foundation. Reprinted by permission of Hazelden Foundation, Center City, MN.

out in class, etc.) to attract attention that they desperately need, albeit in self-defeating ways, and they are receiving little protection from the adults whose patience has worn thin. The characteristics of provocative victims are listed in Box 6.3.

Again, as we reflect on this list, I am sure that many names come to mind. It may be beneficial to reflect, as well, on our reaction to these students, both from the past and the present. Did we try to help them in the past, and what are we doing currently for these kids? It is not uncommon for educators working in schools without a schoolwide plan to address all types of violent behavior in ineffective ways. One of the worst things a staff person can do is suggest that two students involved in a bullying situation work it out themselves. It is not possible for them to do so because there is an imbalance of power to begin with. The victim will continue to be at the mercy of the bully and will have lost any hope for adult intervention. Advising a victim to simply walk away is also poor advice, because the bully may follow and intensify the bullying. The last piece of poor advice is to fight back. Very often, this is just what the bully wants to justify hurting the victim more severely and claiming it was in self-defense (Bitney & Title, 2001).

It is clear from research that addressing bullying behavior assists not only the victim but also the one who bullies. Left untreated, bullying behavior often follows a person into adulthood. There is a strong correlation between bullying behavior as a youth and criminal behavior as an adult. Sixty percent of bullies in Grades 6 to 9 had at least one criminal conviction by age 24 (Banks, 2000, p. 12). Victims of bullying need our help as much as bullies do, because being bullied leads to depression and low self-esteem, which also can follow a person into adulthood.

You've Got To Have a Plan

Educators need to acknowledge that, once again, it is up to them to create a safe environment for all their students. The best way to be successful is to take a whole-school approach. Walker said, "Research shows that schools with low levels of violent behavior are distinguished from those with high levels by the presence of a positive school climate where nurturance, inclusiveness, and a feeling of community are evident" (Walker, 2000, p. 19). Teachers, administrators, all building support staff, and bus drivers need to join forces to assess their school climate and then to develop a unified, consistent plan to ensure that all students are treated fairly and that all students understand the rules and consequences for inappropriate behavior. Consequences should be fair, logical, and consistent for all. School administrators can begin the process by gathering information about the school climate from staff, students, and parents. Tools for doing this are available in programs like No-Bullying Program or Respect and Protect. (See Resource C.) Using this data, staff (and parents) can work together to identify strengths and areas that need improvement. Staff development, strong policies, well-communicated procedures, and constant monitoring of the reporting system will help to ensure that all staff members confront inappropriate or violent behavior in a fair, consistent manner. Students must be able to trust the adults in their school to ensure their safety so that they can focus their energy on learning.

WORKING THE WHEEL

As we discussed in Chapter 4, the brain reacts chemically and the body reacts physically in response to fear or threat. When this happens, the brain loses it ability to access working memory, and it is unlikely that learning will take place. Our goal, then, is to make our classrooms and school environments as safe and nonthreatening as we can. The resiliency wheel is helpful as a guide for creating school and classroom environments in which students can learn and grow without fear. Resiliency-building schools reflect the knowledge that brains on heightened alert cannot focus on learning. Students who feel safe from all forms of violence, low level as well as high level, do better academically. It would be very beneficial to use the resiliency wheel to develop strategies for creating a whole-school approach to nonviolence.

Provide Caring and Support

As resiliency research indicates, the power of one person can never be underestimated. Children who become violent

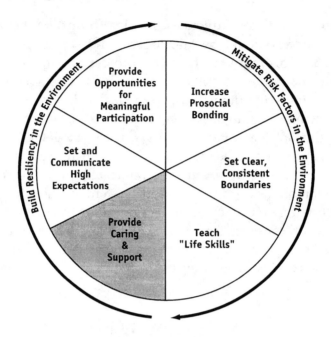

toward others have often felt victimized and rejected themselves. If children who bully and children who are bullied do not get support, they will continue on a dangerous path of violence, aggression, depression, and, possibly retaliation. With support and proper intervention, both bullies and victims can recover successfully. A positive relationship with an adult or an environment that cares and supports all students is key. "When children have a positive, meaningful connection to an adult—whether it be at home, in school, or in the community—the potential for violence is reduced significantly" (Dwyer, Osher, & Warger, 2000, pp. 16-17).

There are many ways for schools to provide caring and support for students. Below are a few ideas. As you think about the strategy of providing caring and support, you will no doubt come up with your own great ideas. Some efforts will be confined to classrooms, and some will be schoolwide. The most effective way to create a safe school is to include the entire school in the effort, including educators, support staff, bus drivers, administrators, parents, and students.

Try This Out With All Ages

■ Create a schoolwide procedure to identify kids who seem troubled or who are engaging in inappropriate behavior. Child study teams or crisis intervention teams are good vehicles for identifying students and referring them for services where appropriate interventions can be planned. I do not mean just special education students, but all students. Staff members sharing ideas and perceptions of particularly worrisome students is helpful in assessing whether or not a student needs assistance. In addition, making other staff members aware of a student who may be having difficulties will increase the possibility that more staff members will notice and intervene to offer help. Sometimes, an intervention may be quite simple, such as inviting a student to join a club, and other times, an outside referral for counseling may be necessary. It may be helpful and relieving to staff to know that more than one of them has noticed the same inappropriate behavior of a student. Only through sharing like this can school staff members join forces to help both bullies and victims.

■ Form Newcomers or Welcome Clubs. These clubs are for established students who want to assist new students in making positive connections. No new student of any age should have to enter a school cafeteria alone. Students who volunteer to be a part of the Newcomers Club need to have preliminary preparation to discuss what it feels like to be new and what things they might do to make it easier for any new students they are assigned to help. It does not work for a principal or counselor to spontaneously ask an established student to help make a new person comfortable. Unless the established student has been prepared for the task, it is likely to be uncomfortable for both students and, therefore, unsuccessful. New students need time to become comfortable, so established students need to understand that initially, this will be a commitment of time and energy. However, once the new student is making friends and adjusting, the established students may not be as needed. Participating students need to be prepared for the separation phase of the intervention as well.

■ Form peer leadership groups. Peer leadership groups at any grade level are very effective for many reasons. First, the peer helpers themselves benefit from contributing to the school climate. Second, the school climate and other students benefit from the things they contribute. Many schools have formed big brothers and big sisters programs where older students adopt younger ones who may be shy or prime candidates for being bullied. Having a relationship with an older student can really help a younger student feel more secure. Maybe offering a student who has shown bullying behavior the opportunity to become a big brother or big sister to someone would help to eradicate the behavior and build empathy. Of course, close supervision and training would be required for the older students.

■ Take pictures. I recently met an elementary school principal who constantly takes pictures of kids doing all sorts of things. She doesn't wait for special occasions. She uses pictures as a way to connect with kids. She will approach a student and say, "I took this picture of you when you were doing . . ., and I thought maybe you would like to have it." The child immediately feels acknowledged and cared about. Offering pictures is a great way to open conversation and make connections to kids. It is especially effective with marginal kids or kids who have had behavior problems, because it is a positive interaction with an authority figure who sees the children and not just the problems they have had. Older students love to get their pictures taken, too. Placing pictures of them (ideally, engaged in a moment of cooperative learning or fun) around the classroom is a great way to communicate how much you treasure time spent with them. One word of caution may be appropriate. Before taking pictures of students, it is always a good idea to get parental permission. Parents usually do not mind, but there may be instances when having a picture taken may be threatening, such as in child custody battles or cases of people escaping domestic violence. Certainly, before sending pictures to any outside place like a newspaper, it is necessary to get written parental permission.

Try This With Elementary Students

■ Create friendship groups. Some students are unpopular because they lack social intelligence and are extremely shy. They don't know how to start conversations, and their interactions are inappropriate. There are many social-skills curricula available to be used in small group sessions with identified youths or in the larger classroom. These can help students learn to interact with others successfully.

Set and Communicate High Expectations

It is clear that failure in school increases young people's risk for engaging in violence and delinquency (Artz, 1998). Students who fall through the cracks, who have little or no parental support, who have undiagnosed learning disabilities or emotional problems, or who just do not value studying and achieving good grades are at considerably higher risk for school failure. Schools need to establish programs to provide the necessary support for these students to be successful. Teachers may need to look beyond the unmotivated behavior to determine if there is another cause for a student's failure to achieve. Every child has an "island of competence," as Brooks (Brooks & Goldstein, 2001) says. We need to find those islands.

> It has to do with finding what is right about kids . . . finding their strengths, finding ways to build them. You don't find kids who are depressed who are extremely good at something, who live their lives around it. None of the murderers we've had are kids who have been very good at something and have led their lives around it. (Seligman, 1998, p. 86)

I would assert that most aggressive, violent kids are kids without belief in their abilities to achieve something positive in life and they are kids without adults who actively believe in them. By that I mean adults who take an interest in them, spend time with them, and take actions that will assist them in being successful in achieving their goals. Educators can make up for this loss by being the ones who communicate to the students that they are capable of achieving high standards and who provide the necessary support for them to do so.

Try This Out With All Ages

■ Take the time to learn about how your students learn best. Discover their strongest intelligences and build with them. Honor your students' learning styles and give choices that will allow students to express their uniqueness. As we discussed in Chapter 3, people appreciate it when another recognizes how they are unique and allows them to express that uniqueness in their work. Use the tools in the appendices of this book to get to know your students better.

■ Offer tutorials. Sit with your students individually to diagnose academic problems and help them create plans to solve them. For example, if students are not turning in homework, instead of simply placing zeros in their homework column, take a few minutes to sit with each one to determine why the homework is not being done. Maybe suggest that you eat lunch together. Then help the student devise a plan to make it up. This communicates to the students that you are invested in their success and not simply in following your policies. Remember that some homes are not conducive to doing homework, and be careful not to overload kids who may be facing difficult family situations at night.

■ Make referrals to psychologists and counselors when you suspect a child is struggling due to learning differences or emotional problems. Follow up and make sure that the child is receiving help. Remember that many students who bully may be engaging in this behavior because they are frustrated by their inability to learn like everyone else. Likewise, many learning-disabled kids get bullied because of their inability to learn like everyone else.

■ Create cross-age tutorials. Older kids assisting younger kids with homework is a win-win for both sides. In addition, allowing students who have struggled to assist others who are younger is a sure way to communicate your belief in their abilities. My son's wise third-grade teacher allowed him to teach other students how to graph numbers with coordinates. Up to this point, my son had been struggling with math and was very discouraged. For some reason, possibly because he is such a visual learner, he picked up graphing easily. This experience boosted his confidence and allowed him to continue to try new tasks. The pride he showed when he told me about the experience was almost palpable.

Provide Opportunities for Meaningful Participation

As we saw in Chapter 5, service learning engages youths in helpfulness and is a great way to build their self-esteem. As important, when others perceive someone to be capable of contributing in meaningful ways, their estimation of that person rises. Many students who are picked on or bullied are not perceived to have high status in anyone's eyes. The same is true for those who bully. Some students need to have teachers or other educators devise ways for them to be seen in a different light. Students will hold those who have opportunities for making meaningful contributions in higher esteem.

Try This Out With All Ages

■ Use cooperative learning. Aronson (Gilbert, 2001), a social psychologist, recommends bringing students together through a cooperative-learning strategy he calls the jigsaw classroom. Students are grouped, and the teacher requires that they work together to solve a problem or create a product of some kind. While students often balk at first, after a while, they begin to work together and often come to appreciate each other's contributions and talents. Aronson said, "The jigsaw classroom is a way to help kids learn from experience that kids who are different from them might have something to offer that's interesting and useful" (cited in Gilbert, 2001, p. 2). I would caution teachers that they need to take care when forming groups, so that a shy, unassertive person is not placed with too many assertive students. Teachers must also prepare carefully so that all students have an important role to perform. Teachers must then carefully monitor and offer assistance only when necessary.

Try This Out With Elementary Students

■ Create special jobs for students to perform. Rotate them fairly so everyone gets a chance. However, there may be a time when special students need to have a job all to themselves in order to be seen by classmates as capable. That is when teachers must get creative and figure out a way to do this. Brooks (Brooks & Goldstein, 2001) tells a story of a young child who did not want to go to school. After his parents dropped him off, he would hide in the bushes in order to postpone the painful entry as long as possible. Brooks advised the principal to find a job for this child, so the principal made him the Caretaker of the Animals. He got a badge to wear that signified his new role and status. Before school each day, it was his job to go to each classroom that had an animal and report back whether there was sufficient food and water and if the cage was clean. As you can imagine, he stopped hiding each day and eagerly did his job with care and commitment. Other students envied his status and viewed him in a very positive light. All it takes is imagination, and educators can come up with many ways for kids to participate in meaningful ways.

Increase Prosocial Bonding

School can be a very enjoyable experience for kids who feel welcome, accepted, understood, and successful. Students who do not feel this way are at great risk. Schools need to develop a culture of tolerance and acceptance for diversity. Schools can create experiences for their students that encourage understanding.

When individuals have accurate information, they are less likely to accept stereotypes and adopt prejudices. As students and educators gain knowledge about other groups and their histories, they become more likely to respect members of those groups and cooperate with them. Drawing attention to the processes of discrimination, engaging actively in team building, and consulting continuously with students all help develop a new culture of tolerance and understanding (Romo, 2000, p. 148).

Try This Out With All Ages

■ One way to acknowledge and celebrate diversity is to have either schoolwide or classroom opportunities for students to describe or show others information about their own traditions and cultures. Making it safe for students to ask one another about their religions, holidays, or family origins will assist students in learning about one another with a deeper appreciation and understanding.

■ Bringing humor into the classroom is a way to lighten the atmosphere and enhance everyone's level of comfort. When people can share a laugh, a bond is immediately formed. Share funny stories about yourself and your experiences. Sometimes, there are books with short, funny anecdotes that you could read before each class to start the day. Encourage students to do the same. Look for the humor in the world because when you do, you almost always find it. Someone once said that you need to have a "Ha! Ha!" before you can have an "Ah! Ha!" Laughter increases oxygen flow, pulse rate, and adrenaline. After a person has this response, the body is more relaxed. Educators can use these times to promote better sociability and learning with their students (Allen, 2001).

■ Be open to students' suggestions and ideas. Doing so increases their feelings of connection to the school. Put suggestion boxes in places where students can easily contribute their ideas. Ask for students to help solve problems. For example, on the morning announcements, the principal could ask: "Many people have complained about the noise in the halls. As you go through the day today, please be thinking of how we could move through the halls more quietly. If you have an idea, please put it in the suggestion box." Be sure to read them and react to them, especially by thanking the students for their ideas. When adults ask for input, listen to it, and discuss it with the students, the students become engaged. Do not ask for input and then ignore it, however, because trust will be broken and relationship damaged.

■ Create rituals. People feel safe and secure when things are predictable. Why not start each class with music to calm the mind? Having students put their heads down and listen to soothing music before class or at the start of a day changes the state of mind and enhances the brain's ability to learn. Maybe asking students to choose soothing music would be helpful and make them more engaged in the activity.

Set Clear and Consistent Boundaries

When addressing violence prevention from a schoolwide perspective, this segment of the wheel becomes extremely important. Students depend on the adults in their schools to protect them, and setting clear and consistent boundaries is one of the best ways to do that. "Researchers are studying and advocating for broader, proactive, positive schoolwide discipline systems that include behavioral support" (Fitzsimmons & Warger, 2000, p. 23). A promising approach for teaching self-discipline and managing behavior is schoolwide behavioral management. In this approach, the emphasis is on behavioral consistency in classrooms as well as in the entire school. Everyone on the school staff is expected to adhere to the policies and procedures decided on. Rather than relying on a specific program, schoolwide behavioral management is a team-based process and schools develop their own individual plans (Fitzsimmons & Warger, 2000).

There are common features of schoolwide behavioral management systems.

1. Total staff commitment to managing student behavior

2. Clearly defined and communicated expectations and rules

3. Clearly stated consequences and procedures for correcting rule-breaking behaviors

4. An instructional component for teaching students self-control, social skills, or both

5. A support plan to address the needs of students with chronic challenging behaviors (Fitzsimmons & Warger, 2000).

Schoolwide efforts are not quick fixes. It can take up to 5 years to fully implement a plan. The process involves assessing the current state of affairs with regard to low and high levels of violence. It is important to involve students in the process and to get staff members on board before moving forward with a plan. Administrative support is critical since teachers will not intervene with students if there is no back-up from the principal or other administrative staff members. To work, a schoolwide approach must be consistent and fair and support the staff members who work to implement it. Schools with schoolwide character education efforts that integrate concepts into curriculum and school policies on behavior are already addressing violence prevention.

Try This Out With All Ages

■ Find out what is happening in your school. Ask students via anonymous surveys to let you know what the culture is like for them. Ask parents, in the same way, to give you their impressions of their children's experiences at school. Ask the staff, including bus drivers and cafeteria workers, the same questions.

■ Place a box in an inconspicuous place where students can easily and confidentially let staff know when they or someone else is having difficulty and need help. Make it safe for students to report issues to authorities.

■ Develop support systems for educators who may need to discuss issues with others in order to deal effectively with classroom or other situations. This would help educators in the same building be consistent with students. Once plans are implemented, have regular meetings to compare notes and discuss issues and progress.

■ Celebrate success. When incidents of low-level aggression are reduced, talk about it and celebrate it. Create a new norm where students know that the norm is to be peaceful and respectful.

■ Use visuals to create the culture where everyone experiences respectfulness. Posters that say things like, "Lincoln Junior High does not welcome put-downs. Be cool, be kind."

Teach Life Skills

Social skills are a key ingredient for lifelong success. People who possess strong social competencies are very resilient. They can interact with others to get their needs met, resolve conflict peacefully, and overcome life's challenges. Many students arrive at school with deficit social skills. As we have said before, they often lack appropriate role models outside school.

Children who achieve in school and develop important reading, critical-thinking, problem-solving, and communication skills are better able to cope with stressful and perhaps dangerous situations. . . . Interventions must begin early to help children develop higher-order thinking skills, empathy, impulse control, anger management, peaceful conflict resolution skills, and assertive communication techniques. (Massey, 2000, p. 7)

Brill (2000b) suggests that we ought to be violence-proofing our students rather than violence-proofing our schools. One way to do this, he asserts, is to assist students, especially those who have been bullied, in developing emotional honesty. This entails owning their emotional pain and dealing effectively with it. He advocates for helping these students to recognize and destigmatize hurt feelings so that they can honor their feelings and come to accept themselves. Brill (2000a) asserts that self-accepting students have no need to seek revenge or engage in destructive (including self-destructive) behavior. They are also more tolerant and accepting of others.

The life skills that seem to be most important for violence prevention have to do with assertiveness, anger management, and conflict resolution. Of course, these are all related to interpersonal and intrapersonal intelligences, or emotional intelligence. And as with all the topics we have dealt with so far in this book, these skills are learned better when they are lived rather than when they are taught. They are learned in schools when educators model them. They are learned best in context when there is an opportunity to practice them. While there are many curricula available to help educators teach social skills (see Resource C), teachers can seize teachable moments throughout the day to highlight many social skills.

Try This Out With All Ages

■ Make it safe to deal with conflict. Teach students how to assert themselves without being offensive. Don't ignore conflict or stop it without both sides being able to resolve it, or it will resurface later in a different form. Peer leaders often make great peer mediators. Schools often adopt peer mediation programs where, with adult supervision, students learn to mediate disputes for other students. When students are properly trained and supervised by trained staff, these programs are very successful.

■ Intervene when you hear inappropriate comments. "When a teacher does not respond to degrading language, students believe that the silence means that the teacher condones those words" (Wessler, 2000/2001, p. 31). When educators speak up against inappropriate comments or language, students are empowered to do so as well.

■ Model the respect for students that you want them to show you. Students come from many different home environments. They may not know that their behavior seems disrespectful to you, especially if they have no role models at home. Something like, "John, when you see me with my hands full of books, please wait before asking me for something. I can't help you until I can free my hands, but then I'd be happy to help. Thanks." This may seems obvious to us, but to kids who are used to being ignored unless they make noise, it is a revelation that someone might actually *want* to help them. They need to learn how to get their needs met without turning off the very people they need.

■ Teach students what bullying behavior looks like so that they can recognize it and do something about it. They need to learn empathy so that they can be sensitive to the feelings of others. (See Resource C for information on No-Bullying Program.)

■ Students of all ages need to learn how to access help for themselves when they need it. Without adult assistance, students have no way to process their hurts and understand them. Too many students suffer silently and, consequently, miss out on a positive school experience. Schools and teachers must make it easy for students to ask for help, safe in the knowledge that things will not get worse as a result. The one thing a teacher or administrator should never do is go to one who bullies and say that someone has complained. To stop bullies, it is necessary to catch them in action and then intervene on behalf of the victim. Bullies need to have their power taken away by adults with the authority to do so. They should never be given any reason to retaliate against a victim who they think got them in trouble.

SUMMARY

Until now, schools have done their best to curb the violence, but too often their efforts have had only limited effect because they have focused primarily on what amounts to be only one or two facets of a multifaceted problem. (Remboldt, 1998, p. 7)

Violence is not an easy problem to solve. Many things contribute to violence in schools but none more than environments where low levels of aggression are tolerated. Schools need a schoolwide, systemic approach to preventing violence of all kinds. Students have the right to go to schools where they feel safe and where they can use their energy to learn and interact in positive ways. Educators can and do create the environments in which students function. They must be sure that their actions do not enable the low-level violence that often escalates into physical forms of aggression. It is important for all educators and school staff members to examine their beliefs about violence, victims, and perpetrators of violence so that they may begin to recognize the events that contribute to it. All educators must accept their responsibility for making schools safe, resiliency-building places for young people to learn and grow.

It is important to remember that those who bully and their victims belong to us and we must help them both. Carol Marshall (personal communication, December 10, 2001), a No-Bullying Program trainer, offers these suggestions:

> If you teach or counsel youth who demonstrate bullying behavior, it is helpful to recognize the need for power that these youth want over others. Provide positive opportunities for all youth to feel powerful, to belong, to feel important, and to contribute without the need to be negative and violent toward other people. Recognize the goals of the youths' negative behavior and plan on ways to react. Face the reasons why youth may have a need for negative attention, revenge, and power. If educators in a school refuse to accept bullying behavior, and enforce nonviolent consequences consistently, potential victims will trust the system of discipline and protection and those who bully will learn that the bullying behavior will not be tolerated anywhere.

Conclusion

Skip Meno, a former school superintendent and current dean of a major college of education, told me that he did not read until sixth grade. I asked how he managed to get to sixth grade without being able to read, and he responded that he was fortunate to come from a family that supported him and that valued education. He said that at home, even at an early age, he was exposed to complex adult conversation. As a result, he possessed a good oral vocabulary that helped him to develop a wonderful system to compensate for his reading problems. Even so, he admits becoming disruptive in school due to his frustration with his apparent inability to read.

Finally, in sixth grade, he was very lucky to have a teacher who did not blame him for his lack of accomplishment but who worked with him after school to find the way to help him. This teacher observed Skip's strengths of vocabulary and verbal expression. It seemed incongruous that an intelligent child who could express himself so well in conversation could not read. He understood the pain and embarrassment that a sixth grader would experience for this apparent failure and approached Skip to offer help. Together, they tried many strategies before finding one that worked. They found success by using sight vocabulary, because they discovered that Skip did not possess phonetic ability. Sounding out words was not a strategy that would work for Skip, so memorization of words seemed to be a better way to go. Before long, Skip began to make great progress. He was reading at ninth-grade level within 6 months.

This teacher, who went on to become a school super-intendent, helped Skip long before the arrival of multiple-intelligences theory. This teacher was successful first, because he believed in every child's ability to learn. Second, he went the extra mile to extend himself to a student who needed help desperately. He unearthed what was standing in Skip's way, found out what strengths Skip possessed, and built on them. Phonemic ability did not appear to be Skip's strong suit, so teaching him to read via other methods was necessary. As Gardner's (1983) theory of multiple intelligences shows, there are many ways to teach people to read or do math.

Those who are lacking in language or math are usually targeted very early in their school careers and labeled, for-mally or informally, so that remediation can take place. As we all know, kids understand the meaning of labels only too well. If they get one, they know that they are somehow not up to par. Unfortunately for these students, teachers can often inter-pret labels the same way. At a very early age, many kids—and teachers—adopt a defeatist attitude that will predict school failure. Thank goodness that Dr. Meno got a teacher with a resiliency attitude instead of a label. In fact, Skip had many resiliency-building factors operating: a supportive family, a persistent teacher with high expectations, success in other performance areas, and the internal desire to do well. Without these factors, his life might have taken a very different turn. Interestingly, the teacher in this scenario was practicing long before either resiliency theory or Gardner's theory was put forth. As Dr. Meno reminded me, most accurate theories come from observation of outstanding practice. His teacher discov-ered and practiced it before Gardner gave it a name.

RESILIENCY IS BEST INTEGRATED INTO WHAT YOU ALREADY KNOW AND DO

When I began to write this book, I thought I might title it *Not One More Thing!* I wanted to acknowledge that even though demands on educators are overwhelming, focusing on building resilient students does not have to be a separate undertaking. Educators who incorporate good educational practice into their daily routines are more likely to produce resilient students as we have just seen. It is common, however, for all the educational megatrends, including resiliency, to be perceived as separate and unrelated. That is why the task of incorporating them into the school day may seem impossible. I hope that this perception has changed after reading this book.

Schools are living, breathing organisms, and some are healthier than others. As I recently heard someone say, "If the fish in the tank are sick, don't blame them, change the water." The healthiest schools appear to have enlightened leadership and a committed staff. In schools like these, kids can't help but be resilient because adults who are resilient surround them. Enlightened administrators recognize, nurture, and celebrate the skills and talents of their staff members. They share ideas as well as control, encourage risk taking, and celebrate accomplishments. Their staff members receive the positive regard that they are expected to give to their students.

The most successful teachers learn to treat the cause of misbehavior or failure and not the misbehavior or failure itself. As we have seen throughout this book, these teachers have the resiliency attitude. Skip Meno learned firsthand that committed teachers do whatever is necessary to ensure their students' success. They believe in each child's ability to learn. They look beyond poor behavior to try to understand what motivates it, and then they look for ways to help the student behave in more productive ways. They are patient. They know that in school, students' needs are more important than their own, and flex to meet those needs. Committed teachers know their students well, set high expectations for (and with) them, and provide the necessary support for their students to be successful.

It would be safe to say that schools carry an unfair load at times, and it would be understandable if educators threw up their hands and said, "Let's look at the home," when problems arise. If only the answer were that simple. I wrote this book so that educators will know that very often they are the lifelines for troubled kids as well as for kids who appear to be model children. Schools can be, and ought to be, places where all kids are respected, protected, nurtured, challenged, and celebrated. Schools ought to prepare kids for more than the SATs and a diploma. Kids ought to leave school understanding themselves: how they are smart, how to manage themselves and their interactions effectively, how they can contribute, and how to live productive lives. Even if they return at the end of the day to bad situations in the home or in the communities in which they live, students can and do hang onto the experiences they have had in school. We have to do everything we can to make those experiences good ones. "Young people frequently forget what we say and do, but they rarely forget how we make them feel" (Carrera, 1996, p. 94).

A LAST WORD ABOUT THE TERM RESILIENT

Recently, I attended a workshop for youth workers on the topic of resiliency. I witnessed a woman struggling with the concept. She wanted to know when a person was considered to be resilient. She wondered how being resilient was any different from just being a good survivor in a bad situation. It was difficult for her to understand how she was supposed to make the youths she was working with, who were already surviving well in high-risk environments, resilient. They are resilient, but they may not know it. I believe that the best thing she can do for those young people is to follow the Wolins' model and make them aware of what they are doing to survive and reframe their behaviors so that they can become aware of them and of how they are resilient.

After many years of working with the concept of resiliency, I have come to understand this: There are seeds of resilience in all of us. Sometimes they get nurtured, and sometimes they do not. Sometimes a person can show incredible strength and resilience in one area of his life and not in another. A child may be a poor student but a wonderful caregiver. A man may be a great teacher but a poor husband. We are all works in progress and, therefore, it is silly to think that at some point in our lives, we ought to be pronounced permanently and totally resilient. Our resiliency is always a work in progress.

The only constant about life, as we all know, is change. Sometimes, we move through life easily, and, at other times, we meet great obstacles. Just when we begin to appreciate our accomplishments, and we feel as if we are on top of our game, life may throw us a curve. We may immediately rise to the occasion and prevail, or we may be shaken to our knees. Only then do we find out how resilient we are. Hopefully, we will be able to stand up again because we can draw from inner strengths acquired from a number of sources: family, friends, our experiences, past successes, faith, and so forth. The ability to bounce back may be there, but it may also take time and energy to be successful. So, although the seeds of resilience are present in all of us, no one is likely to be described as resilient with no possibility of backsliding—unless it is in an epitaph.

Finding resilience in ourselves and in others is a lifelong process. As educators, it is our responsibility to assist students in finding their own strengths and recognizing their own resilience so that, when faced with life's challenges, they can draw from them. This book was intended to be simple. I hesitate to use that word because it may convey that I mean easy when I do not. Good educational practice is not easy. There is no more challenging vocation than to be an educator, whether that means a teacher, counselor, social worker, psychologist, nurse, coach, or administrator. I have tried in this book to offer the essential elements of some very important educational trends so that readers would feel motivated to try some ideas and, hopefully, to learn more about each topic. Clearly, there is overlap among topics, with all of the information related to building resilience in students. I hope that educators who read this book will feel proud of their career choice and inspired to build resilience in every student that they meet.

I wish you all the best with your incredibly important work, and I thank you for all you do to help kids, especially those who need you to be a mirror for them so they see their resilience.

Resource A: Checklist for Assessing Students' Multiple Intelligences

Name of student:_____

Check items that apply.

Linguistic Intelligence

_____Writes better than average for age

_____Spins tall tales or tells jokes and stories

_____Has a good memory for names, places, dates, or trivia

_____Enjoys word games

_____Enjoys reading books

_____Spells words accurately (or, if preschool, does developmental spelling that is advanced for age)

_____Appreciates nonsense rhymes, puns, tongue twisters, etc.

_____Enjoys listening to the spoken word (stories, commentary on the radio, talking books, etc.)

_____Has a good vocabulary for age

_____Communicates to others in a highly verbal way

Other linguistic strengths:

_____

_____

_____

_____

Logical-Mathematical Intelligence

_____Asks a lot if questions about how things work

_____Computes arithmetic problems in his/her head quickly (or, if preschool, math concepts are advanced for age)

_____Enjoys math class (or, if preschool, enjoys counting and doing other things with numbers)

_____Finds math computer games interesting (or, if no exposure to computers, enjoys other math or counting games)

_____Enjoys playing chess, checkers, or other strategy games (or, if preschool, board games requiring counting squares)

_____Enjoys working on logic puzzles or brainteasers (or, if preschool, enjoys hearing logical nonsense such as in *Alice's Adventures in Wonderland*)

_____Enjoys putting things in categories or hierarchies

_____Likes to experiment in a way that shows higher order cognitive thinking processes

_____Thinks on a more abstract or conceptual level than peers

_____Has a good sense of cause-effect for age

Other logical-mathematical strengths:

_____

_____

_____

_____

Spatial Intelligence

_____Reports clear visual images

_____Reads maps, charts, and diagrams more easily than text (or, if preschool, enjoys looking at more than text)

_____Daydreams more than peers

_____Enjoys art activities

_____Draws figures that are advanced for age

_____Likes to view movies, slides, or other visual presentations

_____Enjoys doing puzzles, mazes, "Where's Waldo?" or similar visual activities

_____Builds interesting three-dimensional constructions for age (e.g., Lego buildings)

_____Gets more out of pictures than words when reading

_____Doodles on workbooks, worksheets, or other materials

Other spatial strengths:

_____

_____

_____

_____

Bodily-Kinesthetic Intelligence

_____Excels in one or more sports (or, if preschool, shows physical prowess advanced for age)

_____Moves, twitches, taps, or fidgets while seated for a long time in one spot

_____Cleverly mimics other people's gestures or mannerisms

_____Loves to take things apart and put them back together again

_____Puts his/her hands all over something she/he has just seen

_____Enjoys running, jumping, wrestling, or similar activities (or, if older, will show these interests in a more "restrained" way—e.g., punching a friend, running to class, jumping over a chair

_____Shows skill in craft (e.g., woodworking, sewing, mechanics) or good fine-motor coordination in other ways

_____Has a dramatic way of expressing herself/himself

_____Reports different physical sensations while thinking or working

_____Enjoys working with clay or other tactile experiences (e.g., fingerpainting)

Other bodily-kinesthetic strengths:

_____

_____

_____

_____

Musical Intelligence

_____Tells you when music sounds off-key or disturbing in some other way

_____Remembers melodies of songs

_____Has a good singing voice

_____Plays a musical instrument or sings in a musical choir or other group (or, if preschool, enjoys playing percussion instruments or singing in a group)

_____Has a rhythmic way of speaking and/or moving

_____Unconsciously hums to himself/herself

_____Taps rhythmically on the table or desk as he/she works

_____Sensitive to environmental noises (e.g., rain on the roof)

_____Responds favorably when a piece of music is put on

_____Sings songs that he/she has learned outside the classroom

Other musical strengths:

Interpersonal Intelligence

_____Enjoys socializing with peers

_____Seems to be a natural leader

_____Gives advice to friends who have problems

_____Seems to be street-smart

_____Belongs to clubs, committees, or other organizations (or, if preschool, seems to be part of a regular social group)

_____Enjoys informally teaching other kids

_____Likes to play games with other kids

_____Has two or more close friends

_____Has a good sense of empathy or concern for others

_____Others seek out his/her company

Other interpersonal strengths:

_____

_____

_____

_____

Intrapersonal Intelligence

_____Displays a sense of independence or a strong will

_____Has a realistic sense of his/her strengths and weaknesses

_____Does well when left alone to play or study

_____Marches to the beat of a different drummer in his/her style of living and learning

_____Has an interest or hobby that he/she doesn't talk much about

_____Has a good sense of self-direction

_____Prefers working alone to working with others

_____Accurately expresses how she/he is feeling

_____Is able to learn from his/her failures and successes in life

_____Has high self-esteem

Other intrapersonal strengths:

_____

_____

_____

_____

SOURCE: Armstrong (1994). From *Multiple Intelligences in the Classroom* by Thomas Armstrong. Alexandria, VA: Association for Supervision and Curriculum Development, Copyright © 1994, ASCD. Reprinted by permission. All rights reserved.

Resource B: True Colors Word Sort

DESCRIBE YOURSELF: In the boxes below are groups of word clusters printed *horizontally* in rows. Look at all the boxes in the first row (A, B, C, D). Read the words and decide *which of the four boxes is most like you*. Give that box a 4. Then rank-order the next three boxes from 3 to 1 in descending preference. You will end up with a row of four boxes ranked from 4 (most like you) to 1 (least like you). Now do the next row (E, F ,G, H) and use the same process (4 to 1). Continue with all the rows. You will end up with five horizontal rows that each have a 4, 3, 2, 1.

ROW 1

Active Opportunistic Spontaneous A_____	Parental Traditional Responsible B_____	Authentic Harmonious Compassionate C_____	Versatile Inventive Competent D_____

ROW 2

Curious Conceptual Knowledgeable E_____	Unique Empathic Communicative F_____	Practical Sensible Dependable G_____	Competitive Impetuous Impactful H_____

ROW 3

Loyal Conservative Organized I_____	Devoted Warm Poetic J_____	Realistic Open-minded Adventuresome K_____	Theoretical Seeking Ingenious L_____

ROW 4

Concerned Procedural Cooperative M_____	Daring Impulsive Fun N_____	Tender Inspirational Dramatic O_____	Determined Complex Composed P_____

ROW 5

Philosophical Principled Rational Q_____	Vivacious Affectionate Sympathetic R_____	Exciting Courageous Skillful S_____	Orderly Conventional Caring T_____

Scoring

Add these letters together to discover your strength in each color:

A + H + K + N + S = _____ Orange Score

B + G + I + M + T = _____ Gold Score

C + F + J + O + R = _____ Blue Score

D + E + L + P + Q = _____ Green Score

Total   _____

(Colors should add up to 50)

Circle the highest color, and underline the lowest.

Resource C: Additional Resources

ADDITIONAL RESOURCES
COMPLEMENTING CHAPTER 1

Articles

Benard, B. (Spring, 1997). Focusing therapy on "what families do right": An interview with Steven Wolin, MD. *Resiliency in Action*, pp. 145-150.

Benson, p. (Winter, 1997). Connecting resiliency, youth development, and asset development in a positive-focused framework. *Resiliency in Action*, pp. 117-120.

Bickart, T., & Wolin, S. (1997, November). Practicing resilience in the elementary classroom. *Principal*, pp. 21-24.

Sagor, R. (1996, September). Building resiliency in students. *Educational Leadership*, *54*(1), 38-43.

Tomlinson, C. A. (2000, September). Reconcilable differences? Standards-based teaching and differentiation. *Educational Leadership,* *58*(1), 6-11.

Wang, M., Haertel, G., & Walberg, H. (1997, November). Fostering resilience: What do we know? *Principal,* pp. 18-20.

Wolin, S. (1999, Summer). Easier said than done: Shifting from a risk to a resiliency paradigm. *National Education Service*, pp. 11-14.

Wubbels, T., Levy, J., & Brekelmans, M. (1997, April). Paying attention to relationships. *Educational Leadership,* *54*(7), 82-86.

Organization

Search Institute
Attention: Publications and Survey Information
Thresher Square West
700 South Third Street, Suite 210
Minneapolis, MN 55415-1138
1-800-888-7828

Web Sites

Connect for Kids: www.connectforkids.org (retrieved February 11, 2002)

Resiliency in Action: www.resiliency.com (retrieved February 11, 2002)

Training

Survivor's Pride: Building Resiliency in Youth at Risk (8 videotapes)

AD: Attainment Company, Inc.
P. O. Box 930160
Verone, WI 53593
1-800-327-4269

ADDITIONAL RESOURCES
COMPLEMENTING CHAPTER 2

Articles

Johnson, D., Johnson, R., Stevahn, L., & Hodne, P. (1997, October). The three C's of safe schools. *Educational Leadership, 55*(2), 8-13.

Lewis, C., Schaps, E., & Watson, M. (1996, September). The caring classroom's academic edge. *Educational Leadership, 54*(1), 16-21.

Singh, G. R. (2001, October). How character education helps students grow. *Educational Leadership, 59*(2), 46-49.

Web Sites

Character Education Partnership: www.character.org (retrieved February 11, 2002)

Character Education Network: www.CharacterEd.net (retrieved February 11, 2002)

ADDITIONAL RESOURCES COMPLEMENTING CHAPTER 3

Articles

Campbell, L. (1997, September). How teachers interpret MI theory. *Educational Leadership, 55*(1), 14-19.

Gardner, H. (1997, September). Multiple intelligences as a partner in school improvement. *Educational Leadership, 55*(1), 20-21.

Silver, H., Strong, R., & Perini, M. (1997, September). Integrating learning styles and multiple intelligences. *Educational Leadership, 55*(1), 22-27.

Sweet, S. (1998, November). A lesson learned about multiple intelligences. *Educational Leadership, 56*(3), 50-51.

Tomlinson, C., & Kalbfleisch, M. (1998, November). Teach me, teach my brain: A call for differentiated classrooms. *Educational Leadership, 56*(3), 52-55

Training

True Colors, Inc.
12395 Doherty St.
Riverside, CA 92503
1-800-422-4686
www.truecolors.org (retrieved February 11, 2002)

ADDITIONAL RESOURCES
COMPLEMENTING CHAPTER 4

Articles

Goelitz, J., & Kaiser, J. (2000, Spring). Heart smarts: Developing the head and heart through social and emotional learning. *Reaching Today's Youth*, pp. 25-28.

O'Neil, J. (1996, September). On emotional intelligence: A conversation with Daniel Goleman. *Educational Leadership, 54*(1), 6-11.

Rogers, S., & Renard, L. (1999, September). Relationship-driven teaching. *Educational Leadership, 57*(1), 34-37.

Shelton, C. M. (1999, September). How inner sense builds common sense. *Educational Leadership, 57*(1), 61-64.

Sylwester, R. (2000, November). Unconscious emotions, conscious feelings. *Educational Leadership, 58*(3), 20-24.

Viadero, D. (1996, September 18). Brain trust. *Education Week*, pp. 31-33.

ADDITIONAL RESOURCES
COMPLEMENTING CHAPTER 5

Articles

Cavanaugh, M. P., Johnston, D., Kitay, N., & Yuratovac, S. (1997, April). Learning from 'the big kids." *Educational Leadership, 54*(7), 53-55.

Dundon, B. (2000, January). My voice: An advocacy approach to service learning. *Educational Leadership, 57*(4), 34-37.

Ellis, J., Small-McGinley, J., & DeFabrizio, L. (1999, Summer). 'It's so great to have an adult friend:"A teacher-student mentorship program for at-risk youth. *Reaching Today's Youth*, pp. 46-49.

Web Sites

National Service-Learning Clearinghouse: www.service-learning.org/ (retrieved February 11, 2002)

National Dropout Prevention Center/Network: www. dropoutprevention.org (retrieved February 11, 2002)

Learning In Deed: www.LearningInDeed.org (retrieved February 11, 2002)

ADDITIONAL RESOURCES COMPLEMENTING CHAPTER 6

Articles

Ayers, B., & Hedeen, D. (1996, February). Been there, done that, didn't work: Alternative solutions for behavior problems. *The Best of Educational Leadership, 53*(5), 7-9.

Canada, G. (1999/2000, December/January). Raising better boys. *Educational Leadership, 57*(4),14-17.

Cohen, J. (1999, September). The first 'R': reflective capacities. *Educational Leadership, 57*(1), 70-74.

Goldstein, A. (2000, Winter). Catch it low to prevent it high: Countering low-level verbal abuse. *Reaching Today's Youth,* pp. 10-16.

Hardy, K. (1996, May/June). Breathing room. *Networker*, pp. 53-59.

Johns, B. H. (2000, Winter). The peace-filled classroom: Creating a non-aggressive classroom environment. *Reaching Today's Youth,* pp. 27-31.

Kessler, R. (1999/2000, December/January). Initiation—saying good-bye to childhood. *Educational Leadership, 57*(4), 30-33.

Scherer, M. (1998, May). The shelter of each other: A conversation with Mary Pipher. *Educational Leadership, 55*(8), 6-11.

Stein, N. (1999/2000, December/January). Listening to and learning from girls. *Educational Leadership, 57*(4), 18-20.

Sylwester, R. (1997, February). The neurobiology of self-esteem and aggression. *Educational Leadership, 54*(5), 75-79.

Sylwester, R. (1999, September). In search of the roots of adolescent aggression. *Educational Leadership, 57*(1), 65-69.

VanAcker, R. (2000, Winter). From enraged to engaged: School-based strategies to address student aggression and violence. *Reaching Today's Youth*, pp. 32-39.

Web Sites

Educational Resource Information Center (ERIC): www.eric.ed.gov/ (retrieved February 11, 2002)

Conflict Resolution Educational Network: www.crenet.org (retrieved February 11, 2002), (202-667-9700)

Emotional Health Education: www.emotionalhonesty.com (retrieved February 11, 2002)

Jigsaw Classroom: www.jigsaw.org

Learning Network: www.familyeducation.com (retrieved February 11, 2002)

SaferSanerSchools: www.safersanerschools.org (retrieved February 11, 2002)

Sourthern Poverty Law Center: www.splcenter.org/ teachingtolerance (retrieved February 11, 2002)

Curricula and Training

Get Real About Violence

> AGC/United Learning
> 1560 Sherman Avenue, Suite 100
> Evanston, IL 60201
> 1-800-323-9084

Book and Article

ERIC Review. (2000, Spring). *School Safety: A Collaborative Effort.* (ERIC Document Reproduction Service No. ED 440 640).

Title, B. (1996). *Bully/victim conflict.* Center City, MN: Hazelden Foundation.

References

Allen, R. (August, 2001). Make me laugh: Using humor in the class-room. *Association for Supervision and Curriculum Development Update, (43)*5, 1, 3, 7, 8.

Armstrong, T. (1994). *Multiple intelligences in the classroom.* Alexandria, VA: American Association for Supervision and Curriculum Development.

Artz, S. (1998). *Sex, power, and the violent school girl.* Toronto, Canada: Trifolium Books.

Banks, R. (2000, Spring). School Safety: A Collaborative Effort. *ERIC Review, 7*(1), 12-14. (ERIC Document Reproduction Service No. ED 440 640)

Benard, B. (1991, August). *Fostering resiliency in kids: Protective factors in the family, school and community* (pp. 1-27). Portland, OR: Western Center for Drug-Free Schools and Communities.

Billig, S. H. (2000). Research on K-12 school-based service-learning: The evidence builds. *Phi Delta Kappan, 81*(9), 658-663.

Bitney, J., & Title, B. (2001). The no-bullying program (Rev. ed.). Center City, MN: Hazelden Foundation.

Bocchino, R. (1999). *Emotional literacy: To be a different kind of smart.* Thousand Oaks, CA: Corwin.

Boston, B. (1997). *Service learning: What it offers to students, schools, and communities.* Washington, DC: Council of Chief State School Officers.

Brill, R. (2000a, September). *Education strategies for preventing violence.* Workshop presented at the Fifth National Conference on Advancing School-Based Mental Health Programs, Atlanta, GA.

Brill, R. (2000b). *Emotional honesty and self-acceptance.* Philadelphia: Xlibris.

Brooks, R., & Goldstein, S. (2001). Raising resilient children. Chicago, IL: Contemporary Books.

Carrera, M. (1996). *Lesson for lifeguards*. New York: Donkey Press.

Character Education Partnership (CEP). (1996). *Character education in U.S. schools: A new consensus.* Alexandria, VA: Author.

Checkley, K. (1997, September). The first seven . . . and the eighth. *Educational Leadership, 55*(1), 8-13.

Cobb, C. D., & Mayer, J. D. (2000, November). Emotional intelligence: What the research says. *Educational Leadership, 58*(3), 14-18.

Conrad, D., & Hedin, D. (1991, June). School-based community service: What we know from research and theory. *Phi Delta Kappan, 72*(10), 749.

Dwyer, K., Osher, D., & Warger, C. (2000, Spring). Warning signs of violence. *ERIC Review, 7*(1), 16-17. (ERIC Document Reproduction Service No. ED 440 640)

Fitzsimmons, M. K., & Warger, C. (2000, Spring). Schoolwide behavioral management systems. *ERIC Review 7*(1), 23-24. (ERIC Document Reproduction Service No. ED 440 640)

Frankl, V. (1959). *Man's search for meaning*. New York: Simon & Schuster.

Gardner, H. (1983). *Frames of mind: The theory of multiple intelligences*. New York: Basic Books.

Gardner, H. (1997, September). Multiple intelligences as a partner in school improvement. *Educational Leadership*, 20-21.

Garmezy, N., & Rutter, M. (1983). *Stress, coping, and development in children.* New York: McGraw-Hill.

Gilbert, S. (2001, March). No one left to hate: Averting Columbines. Retrieved from *The New York Times on the Web*, April 17, 2002.

Goleman, D. (1995). *Emotional intelligence.* New York: Bantam.

Hanson, J. R., & Dewing, T. (1990). *Research on the profiles of at-risk learners: Research monograph series.* Moorestown, NJ: Institute for Studies in Analytic Psychology.

Hawkins, J. D., Catalano, R. F., & Miller, J. Y. (1992). Risk and protective factors for alcohol and other drug problems. *Psychological Bulletin, 112*(1), 64-105.

Hazelden Foundation. (1999). *Respect and protect violence prevention and intervention.* Center City, MN: Author.

Henderson, N. (1999). Preface. In N. Henderson, B. Benard, & N. Sharp-Light (Eds.), *Resiliency in action: Practical ideas for*

*overcoming risks and building strengths in youth, families, &
communities,* (pp. v-vi). San Diego, CA: Resiliency In Action.

Henderson, N., & Milstein, M. (1996). *Resiliency in schools: Making it
happen for students and educators.* Thousand Oaks, CA: Corwin.

Higgins, G. O. (1994). *Resilient adults: Overcoming a cruel past.*
San Fransisco: Jossey-Bass.

Kirby, D. (2001, May). *Emerging answers: Research findings on
programs to reduce teen pregnancy.* Washington, DC: National
Campaign to Prevent Teen Pregnancy.

Kohn, A. (1997, February). How not to teach values. *Phi Delta
Kappan*, 429-437.

Krystal, S. (1998/1999, December/January). The nurturing potential
of service learning. *Educational Leadership*, pp. 58-61.

Lickona, T. (1991). *Educating for character: How our schools can
teach respect and responsibility.* New York: Bantam.

Lickona, T. (1998, February). A more complex analysis is needed.
Phi Delta Kappan, 449-454.

MacLean, P. (1990). *The triune brain in evolution.* New York: Plenum.

Massey, M. S. (2000). *The effects of violence on young children.* The
ERIC Review: School safety: A collaborative effort. Volume 7,
Issue 1, 6-8 (NLE 2000-4403).

Melchior, A. (1999). *Summary report: National evaluation of Learn
and Serve America.* Waltham, MA: Center for Human Resources,
Brandeis University.

Mendler, A. N. (2000). *Motivating students who don't care.*
Bloomington, IN: National Educational Service.

Mitchell, K. (2000, Spring). How safe is my child's school? *ERIC
Review, (7)*1, 2-4. (ERIC Document Reproduction Service
No. ED 440 640)

National Society for Experiential Education. (1994). *Partial list of
experiential learning terms and their definitions.* Raleigh, NC:
Author.

O'Hanlon, W., & Davis, M. (1989). *In search of solutions: A new
direction in psychotherapy.* New York: Norton.

Peele, S. (1986, September). The "cure" for adolescent drug abuse:
Worse than the problem? *Journal of Counseling and Development*, 65, 23-24.

Pines, M. (1984, Fall). Resilient children: The search for protective
factors. *American Educator, 8*(3), 34-37.

Poole, C. (1997, May). Up with emotional health. *Educational Leadership*, 12-14.

Remboldt, C. (1998). *Violence in schools: The enabling factor.* Center City, MN: Hazelden Foundation.

Romo, H. D. (2000, Spring). Improving ethnic and racial relations in the schools. *ERIC Review 7*(1), 25-26. (ERIC Document Reproduction Service No. ED 440 640)

Rutter, M. (1984, March). Resilient children. *Psychology Today*, 57-65.

Saleebey, D. (Ed.). (1997). *The strengths perspective in social work practice.* New York: Addison-Wesley Longman.

Salovey, P., & Mayer, J. D. (1990). Emotional intelligence. *Imagination, Cognition and Personality, 9*(3), 185-211.

Sarason, S. (1990). *The predictable failure of educational reform.* San Francisco: Jossey-Bass.

Search Institute. (1997). *The asset approach: Giving kids what they need to succeed.* Minneapolis, MN: Author.

Seligman, M. (1998). *Developing a science of strengths: The key to preventing youth violence and other problems.* Speech at the National Press Club, September 3, 1998. Retrieved February 17, 2002, from www.apa.org/releases/epidemic.html

Shumer, R. (2000, April). Service and citizenship: A connection for the future. *High School Magazine, 7*(8), 34.

Silver, H., Strong, R., & Perini, M. (2000). *So each may learn: Integrating learning styles and multiple intelligences.* Alexandria, VA: Association for Supervision and Curriculum Development.

Tai-Seale, T. (2000). Service-learning: Historical roots, present forms, and educational potential for training health educators. *Journal of Health Education, 31*(5), 256-261.

Tell, C. (1999/2000, December/January). Generation what? Connecting with today's youth. *Educational Leadership, 57*(4), 8-13.

True Colors, Inc. (1996). *Training material.* Riverside, CA: Author.

Walker, D. (2000, Spring). School violence prevention. *ERIC Review, 7*(1), 18-20. (ERIC Document Reproduction Service No. ED 440 640)

Werner, E., & Smith, R. (1989). *Vulnerable but invincible: A longitudinal study of resilient children and youth.* New York: Adams, Bannister, & Cox. (Original work published 1982)

Wessler, S. (2000/2001, December/January). Sticks and stones. *Educational Leadership, 58*(6), 28-33.

Westat, R. (1999). Service-learning and community services in K-12 public schools. *National Center for Education Statistics: Statistics in Brief,* (NCES 1999-043). Washington, DC: U.S. Department of Education.

Wolfe, P. (2001). *Brain matters: Translating research into classroom practice.* Alexandria, VA: Association for Supervision and Curriculum Development.

Wolin, Steven, & Wolin, Sybil. (1993). *The resilient self: How survivors of troubled families rise above adversity.* New York: Villard.

Wolin, Steven, & Wolin, Sybil. (1994). *Survivor's pride* [videotapes]. Verona, WI: Attainment Company.

Index

**CORWIN
PRESS**

The Corwin Press logo—a raven striding across an open book—represents the happy union of courage and learning. We are a professional-level publisher of books and journals for K-12 educators, and we are committed to creating and providing resources that embody these qualities. Corwin's motto is "Success for All Learners."